Discovering CONNECTIONS

A Guide to the Fun of Bridging Disability Differences

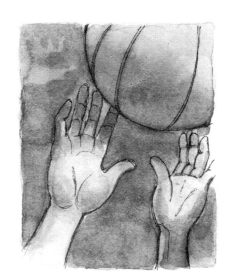

Discovering CONNECTIONS

A Guide to the Fun of Bridging Disability Differences

by Linda D. Hill

with the Cowichan Valley Independent Living Resource Centre

Published by

BUILDING
BRIDGES

Published by:

Building Bridges
P.O. Box 156, Duncan, BC, Canada, V9L 3X3
Phone or Fax : 1-250-746-1529 or
in Canada and USA phone or fax toll free: 1-888-746-1529
TTY: 1-250-746-1539
E-mail: BRIDGES@ISLAND.NET
Visit our web page at: http://www.island.net/~bridges/

Book and cover design by Kim Barnard, Graphic Details
Cover illustrations and community recreation illustrations by Ian Finlayson
Circle drawings by David and Faye Wetherow, and Ariane Templeton

Printed in Victoria, BC, Canada, 1998

Canadian Cataloguing in Publication Data

Hill, Linda, 1954-
    Discovering connections

    Includes bibliographical references.
    ISBN 0-9683284-0-7 (lay-flat binding)
    ISBN 0-9683284-1-5 (3-hole punch)

    1. Handicapped—Social conditions. 2. Handicapped—Recreation.
    3. Handicapped—Attitudes. 4. Socialization.
    I. Cowichan Valley Independent Living Resource Centre. II. Title.
    HV3011.H54 1998   362.4   C98-910154-1

February 21, 1972 – July 16, 1983

Dedicated to Chantel Harper —

during your journey across to the other side
you stopped long enough
to build a bridge to my soul.

Table of Contents

Building Bridges
Box 156, Duncan, British Columbia, CANADA V9L 3X3
Phone or fax toll free: 1-888-746-1529 TTY: 1-250-746-1539

BUILDING BRIDGES

©1998 Linda D. Hill
Please obtain permission from the publisher to copy any page.
Building Bridges
Box 156, Duncan, British Columbia, CANADA V9L 3X3
Phone or fax toll free: 1-888-746-1529 TTY: 1-250-746-1539

BUILDING
BRIDGES

Notes From The Publisher:

Travelling Beyond Disability Definitions

We are often asked which disabilities this book is about. Our answer is that this travel guide includes everyone who communicates, or is learning to communicate, through the universal language of fun. You are invited on these journeys no matter what disabilities you have or don't have. The focus is on enjoying diversity and on mutual learning. As you discover more and more connections with each other and your community, you will learn a great deal about disability issues as well as access, equity, and inclusion issues. We look forward to learning of your experiences with this guidebook and finding out more about connections you have discovered. You are welcome to phone, fax, write, or e-mail us with your questions, ideas, and stories.

To Photocopy Or Not To Photocopy? A Common Dilemma

At **Building Bridges**, we are pleased and proud to have published a book for people to share with others. If you ask, we will readily give you permission to copy a few pages for personal or educational use so long as you acknowledge **Linda Hill** and **Building Bridges**. At the same time, please remember that this book is copyrighted and that a number of non-profit societies raise funds through book sales. We ask you to respect this right of ownership by purchasing additional copies of *Discovering Connections* if you want to reproduce or otherwise use more than a few pages. You can purchase *Discovering Connections* from a disability organization in your community, from your local bookstore, or you can contact **Building Bridges** directly. We have discounts for purchasers ordering ten or more copies of this book, including substantial discounts for educators and facilitators who want each member of a class or group to have a copy.

You can also raise funds for your organization while educating your community about the fun of bridging disability differences. Selling *Discovering Connections* is an excellent fund-raising opportunity for non-profit societies and other groups with an interest in disability issues. In Canada and USA Call or Fax Toll Free 1-888-746-1529 or e-mail us at bridges@island.net for more information.

Building Bridges
P.O. Box 156, Duncan, BC, Canada, V9L 3X3
Phone or Fax : 1-250-746-1529 or
in Canada and USA phone or fax toll free: 1-888-746-1529
TTY: 1-250-746-1539
E-mail: BRIDGES@ISLAND.NET
Visit our web page at: http://www.island.net/~bridges/

Acknowledgements

I am thankful for many journeys that have helped me discover ways of connecting across differences. Travels with my foster brother have provided constant lessons about the realities of growing up with disabilities, the meaning of unconditional love, and the challenges of interdependence. More than twenty years of community development work in the Deaf community and with Hearing parents of Deaf children has taught me a great deal about cross-cultural communication as well as the power of shared laughter in building trust between people who speak different languages. These two journeys, as well as university studies, have provided a strong base for hundreds of adventures bringing children and adults together to reach across ability, communication, and cultural differences to make meaningful connections. This guidebook has also been greatly influenced by several years living and travelling in the South Pacific where socializing and giving time to people are far more important than accomplishing tasks or accumulating things.

Some of the many, many people and organizations I would like to thank for guiding me on my journeys include:

> my husband and soul mate, **John Scull**, who has explored so many new places and different cultures with me, who loves me for who I am, and who encouraged me to get this book off the backburner

> everyone in my family, especially my amazing Mom, **Diana Hill** and my foster brother, **Michael Jacobsen**

> my friends and colleagues from the Island Deaf and Hard of Hearing Centre and the South Vancouver Island Association of the Deaf, especially **Becky Hoodless**, the **Golinskys**, the **Gordons**, and the **Walcots**

> people who have participated in and organizations that have sponsored Building Bridges Across Differences programs, especially Cowichan Valley Independent Living Resource Centre (CVILRC): your members transformed my ideas about integration into a philosophy of inclusion. A special thank you to **Cathy La France** and **Deb Thorne** of the CVILRC for your encouragement and assistance with editing many, many rough drafts of this book

> everyone who welcomed me during my short two years helping to develop Community Based Rehabilitation in the Solomon Islands but especially **John Wesley Panda** and **Leonard Williams** of the Disabled Persons Rehabilitation Association, and **Diana Yates** of the Ministry of Health and Medical Services Rehabilitation Division

To all of my family, friends, colleagues, and teachers: I thank you from the bottom of my heart for your many gifts.

Linda D. Hill, Ph.D.
Registered Psychologist

Preface

Discovering Connections is based on a course called *Rebuilding Fun Into Life* where people come together for fun, learning and community participation. I first learned about *Rebuilding Fun Into Life* courses in 1991 when the Cowichan Valley Independent Living Resource Centre was in its early stages of development. Linda had approached us at the Centre and asked whether we would be interested in sponsoring a Facilitator's Training Institute for our community. I agreed to participate myself as a facilitator trainee.

Once I became involved in the course, I found myself truly having fun within a setting that promoted equality, full inclusion, and mutual learning for everyone regardless of their educational background or abilities. I quickly saw the potential for this course to form the foundation of our Peer Support program. The ideas that promoted acceptance and understanding of diversity appealed to me most because they appeared to complement the Independent Living philosophy of our Centre.

We have continued to offer *Rebuilding Fun Into Life* courses on a bi-annual basis, often in partnership with our local community centre. The concepts underpinning the course have now become an integral part of the Cowichan Valley Independent Living Resource Centre's practices. With Linda's help, we have assisted agencies (including our own) in taking concrete steps toward becoming inclusive. I have also had the opportunity to work with Linda to provide facilitator training in another community, Thunder Bay, Ontario.

Many people make major changes in their lives as a result of their experiences with *Discovering Connections*. Some have become more active in their community and have developed long lasting friendships. Others have taken smaller steps toward exploring their community. Whatever the case might be, those who get involved come away saying that it has been the most FUN they have ever experienced. So please take the time to explore this travel guide, enjoy the trip, and discover the land of inclusion.

Cathy La France

Cathy La France, Executive Director
Cowichan Valley Independent Living Resource Centre

Building Bridges
Box 156, Duncan, British Columbia, CANADA V9L 3X3
Phone or fax toll free: 1-888-746-1529 TTY: 1-250-746-1539

Section 1:

Background To Discovering Connections

"We come together in dignity,
bringing our gifts to share.
Finding places we've never been
and bringing our new friends there."

— Susan, Donald, Estella, and Sherry, 1996

©1998 Linda D. Hill
Please obtain permission from the publisher to copy any page.
Building Bridges
Box 156, Duncan, British Columbia, CANADA V9L 3X3
Phone or fax toll free: 1-888-746-1529 TTY: 1-250-746-1539

BUILDING
BRIDGES

Bridging Disability Differences

My thoughts...
· ·
· ·
· ·
· ·
· ·
· ·
· ·
· ·
· ·
· ·
· ·
· ·
· ·
· ·
· ·
· ·
· ·
· ·
· ·
· ·
· ·
· ·
· ·
· ·

Some people try to avoid differences by staying apart and only associating with people who are the same as they are.

Some people try to eliminate differences by helping people who are different become the same as everyone else.

Some people try to build bridges across differences by learning about each other from each other.

Building Bridges
Box 156, Duncan, British Columbia, CANADA V9L 3X3
Phone or fax toll free: 1-888-746-1529 TTY: 1-250-746-1539

BUILDING BRIDGES

Who Is This Guidebook For?

Discovering Connections is a guidebook for everyone who wants to explore ways of bridging disability differences to make meaningful connections with each other and with our communities. This is a book for:

➤ people with disabilities

➤ family members, friends, and neighbours of people with disabilities

➤ professionals, volunteers, and students

➤ anyone who enjoys getting to know people from different backgrounds

My thoughts...

We are building communities where we are enriched by our differences as well as our similarities. Accepting, understanding, supporting, and enjoying each other is what *Discovering Connections* is all about.

Building Bridges
Box 156, Duncan, British Columbia, CANADA V9L 3X3
Phone or fax toll free: 1-888-746-1529 TTY: 1-250-746-1539

What Is This Guidebook About?

Take a moment to imagine setting out on a voyage of discovery with people from various backgrounds:

My thoughts...

....
....
....
....
....
....
....
....
....
....
....
....
....
....
....
....
....
....
....
....
....
....
....

Some of you have disabilities and some of you, at this point in your lives, don't. You each have various reasons for wanting to connect, as well as different hopes and fears about what you will discover as you explore your community together. Although you've heard that these travels can be a lot of fun, none of you knows quite what to expect or what you will encounter along the way.

Some of you know a few people and some of you don't know anyone. At first, some of you stand out because of physical differences or because of differences in how you communicate or interact. Some of you are feeling shy or nervous or even scared. Luckily, your group has a few experienced travellers who are already good at connecting across differences. After a few jokes and introductions everyone begins to relax and enjoy the changing scenery.

As you get to know each other, your first impressions fade to the background and soon you are discovering what talents, gifts, and amazing life stories each person has brought along to make the trip interesting and fun. Together you are discovering new places to go and enjoying new experiences, right in your own community.

By the end of your explorations, you have come to know each other well and you are more aware of ways to get involved in your community. Each of you has become more open to bridging all kinds of differences and supporting others to get involved. Along the way you have been educating everyone you meet about how to make communities more inclusive. A few of you have formed friendships that will continue long after the voyage ends. Some of you are eager to get another group of people together and go exploring all over again.

©1998 Linda D. Hill
Please obtain permission from the publisher to copy any page.
Building Bridges
Box 156, Duncan, British Columbia, CANADA V9L 3X3
Phone or fax toll free: 1-888-746-1529 TTY: 1-250-746-1539

BUILDING
BRIDGES

Different Destinations

People have various destinations in mind when they get together with others to discover ways of bridging disability differences. You may want to:

- get more active

- meet new people

- help people find out what they have to give

My thoughts...

- clear up misconceptions and reduce prejudices about disabilities

- learn more about community resources and possibilities for participation

- break down barriers between people who have professional qualifications and people who have disability labels

- build self esteem

- bridge gaps and overcome barriers that prevent some people from getting involved in their community

- do more socializing and communicating

- help a school, work-place, neighbourhood, or community organization become more welcoming of people with disabilities

- explore some ways of developing new friendships

- experience something new and different

- _____
  _____
  _____

- _____
  _____
  _____

- _____
  _____
  _____

Bridging disability differences is much like bridging cultural differences. You will experience personal and social change similar to the changes people bring home from world travels.

Stages Of Discovery

We are all at different stages of discovering ways of bridging disability differences:

My thoughts...

....

....

....

....

....

....

....

....

....

....

....

....

....

....

....

....

....

....

....

....

....

....

....

....

....

....

> Perhaps you feel uncomfortable around people with disabilities or around people who have certain types of disabilities. At this stage, reading through this guidebook will help you relax and feel more comfortable about connecting across differences.

> You may be thinking about possible ways you might reach across differences that separate you or someone you care about from full and active participation in the community. At this stage, reading this guidebook will help you decide what steps you could take and what directions you could go.

> You may be preparing to get together with some different people to explore the fun of bridging differences. If so, this guidebook will help you find fellow travellers and will help you plan enjoyable journeys to take together.

> If you are at the stage where you are already actively involved in exploring community connections, this book will give you more ideas for ways of bringing different people together to explore with you.

> If you are a member or leader of a diverse group of people who are bridging disability differences, you can use this guidebook as a participants' manual.

BUILDING BRIDGES

©1998 Linda D. Hill
Please obtain permission from the publisher to copy any page.
Building Bridges
Box 156, Duncan, British Columbia, CANADA V9L 3X3
Phone or fax toll free: 1-888-746-1529 TTY: 1-250-746-1539

Levels Of Connecting

Getting to know each other is safe, fun, and comfortable so long as we connect on the same level.

➤ Almost all of us are strangers. We are not personally connected at all with most of the millions and millions of people in the world.

➤ Most of the people we connect with are acquaintances. This is a light and easy level of connecting with no commitment beyond being polite and respectful to each other.

➤ Some of our acquaintances become buddies. This is a deeper level of connecting where we find out that we have some things in common that we enjoy doing together.

➤ A few of our buddies become personal friends. Friends enjoy doing things together, talking together, sharing with each other, and helping each other out.

➤ Once in a while a friend becomes so close that you feel as if you have known each other your entire life. When a friendship connects at a level that feels like family, you can turn to each other for help and support whenever needed.

➤ Very rarely, perhaps only once in a life-time (and perhaps never), a personal friend becomes an intimate partner.

Friendships and intimate relationships are deep connections with potential for great sorrow as well as great joy. Risks of disappointment, exploitation, and burn-out in new relationships can be avoided by connecting at the lighter levels and by practicing the connecting skills described in Section 4 of this guidebook. Although there are no guarantees of lasting friendships, these deeper connections have more chance to grow when:

➤ the pace is relaxed and slow

➤ the focus is on enjoyment and mutual learning

➤ we treat each other with respect and consideration

My thoughts...

©1998 Linda D. Hill
Please obtain permission from the publisher to copy any page.
Building Bridges
Box 156, Duncan, British Columbia, CANADA V9L 3X3
Phone or fax toll free: 1-888-746-1529   TTY: 1-250-746-1539

BUILDING BRIDGES

Section 2:
Travel Preparations

"Every person has something unique to share
that will benefit another person.
We have to provide opportunities for
this to happen."

— Jack, 1996

©1998 Linda D. Hill
Please obtain permission from the publisher to copy any page.
Building Bridges
Box 156, Duncan, British Columbia, CANADA V9L 3X3
Phone or fax toll free: 1-888-746-1529 TTY: 1-250-746-1539

Keeping A Travel Journal

J ournal pages with questions about the connections you are discovering will get you actively involved in thinking about the ideas in this guidebook. We invite you to be creative in keeping a journal. You could write, doodle, draw, or paint on these journal pages or you could:

My thoughts...

....
....
....
....
....
....
....
....
....
....
....
....
....
....
....
....
....
....
....
....
....
....
....
....

➤ make a scrap book or an album

➤ keep a diary

➤ collect souvenirs of your explorations in the community

➤ jot notes and sketches on scraps of paper

➤ draw, paint, or colour pictures

➤ make collages

➤ make videos

➤ compose music or poetry

➤ come up with your own creative way of keeping a journal

➤ _____

➤ _____

➤ _____

You may want to keep your own journal, or several of you may want to keep a journal together.

BUILDING BRIDGES
©1998 Linda D. Hill
Please obtain permission from the publisher to copy any page.
Building Bridges
Box 156, Duncan, British Columbia, CANADA V9L 3X3
Phone or fax toll free: 1-888-746-1529 TTY: 1-250-746-1539

Journal Page

Use this first journal page to think about what you have learned so far.

My thoughts...

Idea Starters

What connections do you hope to discover in your community?

We are all at different stages of bridging disability differences. What stage are you at?

Building Bridges
Box 156, Duncan, British Columbia, CANADA V9L 3X3
Phone or fax toll free: 1-888-746-1529 TTY: 1-250-746-1539

BUILDING BRIDGES

Finding Travelling Companions

Unlike most books that can be read alone, *Discovering Connections* is a book for several people to read together. Showing this guidebook to people will make networking easy.

You will begin *discovering connections* as soon as you get together with just one or two interested people from different backgrounds.

My thoughts...

....
....
....
....
....
....
....
....
....
....
....
....
....
....
....
....
....
....
....
....
....

Think first about the people you are already connected with through family, friends, work, school, or leisure. Next, think about people who work, volunteer, or participate in programs, offices, or agencies that deal with disability issues. Now, expand your thinking beyond people you know and people who are directly involved with disability issues. *Discovering Connections* will also be of interest to people involved in counselling, educating, peace building, and co-operative learning. People who like to travel will be intrigued by the ideas in *Discovering Connections* as well as people who are active in civil rights, church, community development, health promotion, multicultural programs, or anti-racism work. Here is a list of the kinds of people, groups, and organizations you could contact:

➤ family members and friends

➤ places where you volunteer, work, or go to school

➤ disability groups and organizations

➤ government offices

➤ businesses that are making an effort to be accessible to people with disabilities

➤ professional service providers

➤ service clubs and other community organizations

➤ churches

➤ community centres

➤ staff and students at schools, community colleges, or universities

➤ literacy programs

➤ groups, clubs, and organizations that have a special interest in people, the environment, cross-cultural communication, or community health

Best of luck in gathering a diverse mixture of people who are interested in exploring the fun of bridging disability differences.

BUILDING BRIDGES

Building Bridges
Box 156, Duncan, British Columbia, CANADA V9L 3X3
Phone or fax toll free: 1-888-746-1529 TTY: 1-250-746-1539

Journal Page

Who else could you show this book to? List all your ideas here and then select the people or places that seem easiest for you to connect with. After you get in touch with some people, come back to this journal page and record what happened.

My thoughts...

Idea Starters

who else could you show this book to?

what barriers make it hard for people from different backgrounds to get together to discover connections?

what supports make it easy for people from different backgrounds to get together to discover connections?

Building Bridges
Box 156, Duncan, British Columbia, CANADA V9L 3X3
Phone or fax toll free: 1-888-746-1529 TTY: 1-250-746-1539

BUILDING BRIDGES

Getting Packed For Your Journeys

Have you packed your spirit of adventure and your sense of humour? Are you willing to reach across different ways of communicating, behaving, learning, experiencing, and seeing the world? Are you looking forward to learning from people who come from different backgrounds? If so, then you are ninety-nine percent packed already.

All of the journeys in this guidebook are free or very inexpensive, so you need little or no money. Bringing food and refreshments to share is always a good way to relax and get to know each other better. The most important thing to bring is an open mind.

The armchair travelling activities in this guidebook encourage artistic expression through drawing, painting, sculpting, drama, and other expressive art forms. You will want to bring your creative energy as well as some art supplies such as:

➤ large sheets of newsprint

➤ scissors

➤ painting or drawing supplies

➤ glue

➤ old magazines

➤ photographs

➤ props and costumes

➤ _____

➤ _____

➤ _____

Don't worry if you don't feel completely prepared yet. One of the best things about exploring connections in your own community is that you can easily go home to get anything you have forgotten.

My thoughts...

. . . .
. . . .
. . . .
. . . .
. . . .
. . . .
. . . .
. . . .
. . . .
. . . .
. . . .
. . . .
. . . .
. . . .
. . . .
. . . .
. . . .
. . . .
. . . .
. . . .
. . . .

©1998 Linda D. Hill
Please obtain permission from the publisher to copy any page.
Building Bridges
Box 156, Duncan, British Columbia, CANADA V9L 3X3
Phone or fax toll free: 1-888-746-1529 TTY: 1-250-746-1539

Journal Page

What can you bring with you to help make these journeys more enjoyable for you and the people you are getting together with?

My thoughts . . .

Idea Starters

You could think of:
- things you could bring such as food and supplies
- ways you could help such as contacting people, getting things ready, or cleaning up
- skills you have to offer such as leadership and support skills
- co-operative games to play
- art, music, writing, or dramatic talents
- special qualities such as the ability to try new things or to laugh
- knowledge about community events, places to go, and activities to participate in

©1998 Linda D. Hill
Please obtain permission from the publisher to copy any page.
Building Bridges
Box 156, Duncan, British Columbia, CANADA V9L 3X3
Phone or fax toll free: 1-888-746-1529 TTY: 1-250-746-1539

Making The Commitment To Travel Together

Just as it can be difficult to get around to making holiday reservations, making the commitment to begin meeting together to explore ways of bridging disability differences can be a real challenge. It seems that almost everyone who thinks about bridging differences experiences a mixture of hopes, fears, and unanswered questions at first.

Here is what a few people have told us:

My thoughts...

. . . .
. . . .
. . . .
. . . .
. . . .
. . . .
. . . .
. . . .
. . . .
. . . .
. . . .
. . . .
. . . .
. . . .
. . . .
. . . .
. . . .
. . . .
. . . .
. . . .
. . . .
. . . .
. . . .

> *"The morning of the first day I thought, 'This is never going to work. We are coming from such different backgrounds.' By noon the second day we had blended together so well it was a complete turn-around."* (Suzanne, 1995)

> *"By the end, everybody seemed to be very comfortable with each other. This was a marked improvement from the beginning when everybody was scared stiff. I really enjoyed myself."* (Anne, 1989)

> *"At first I thought to myself, 'I don't know what I'm doing here'. Some of the people there struck me as being a little off centre and I hadn't expected it. But after the first day it was great."* (Judi, 1994)

The more supportive you are of each other in these early planning stages, the more you will each experience success in bridging disability differences. These successes will help you continue getting together to explore ways of connecting with each other and with your community.

Journal Page

What are your thoughts about making a commitment to get together with others to reach across disability differences?

My thoughts...

Idea Starters

What are your fears about the journeys ahead?

What are your hopes about the connections you will discover in your community?

Building Bridges
Box 156, Duncan, British Columbia, CANADA V9L 3X3
Phone or fax toll free: 1-888-746-1529 TTY: 1-250-746-1539

BUILDING BRIDGES

Finding Time To Get Together

Each of the ten journeys in this guidebook involves at least two meetings. The first meeting of each journey is a group meeting where you read the guidebook together, try out an armchair travelling activity, and make community connecting plans. The second meeting is when you go out together to do something fun in the community.

The time commitment is two or three hours per meeting, so each journey will involve four to six hours of your time. If you go on all ten journeys you will be spending between forty and sixty hours *discovering connections* together. People have chosen several different ways of scheduling this amount of time. You could:

➤ get together once a week for twenty weeks (five months)

➤ get together twice a week for ten weeks (two and a half months)

➤ spend one full week together going on two journeys each day

➤ get together for two or three weekends in a row and go on four or five journeys during each weekend

➤ _____

➤ _____

➤ _____

My thoughts...

....
....
....
....
....
....
....
....
....
....
....
....
....
....
....
....
....
....
....
....
....
....
....
....

"*The meetings followed a similar pattern to the first one. At the beginning of the sessions we would go over new skills. We did this in a circle and everybody would get a chance to contribute to the discussion. Afterwards we would do a creative activity to practice these skills. Then we would have a coffee break where we would discuss our plans for the following week. Everybody would go back to the group and then the action plans were shared. We went shopping for Christmas presents, sewed Christmas stockings, got together at a restaurant for coffee, went for walks in Beacon Hill park, went for drives, and went to my place to talk. I even held a surprise birthday party at my place.*" (Anne, 1989)

Finding A Place To Meet

You will want to find a comfortable meeting place to get together. For the first meeting of each journey you need a setting where you have the time, space, and privacy to read and discuss the ideas in the book together and then try out the suggested armchair travelling activities. You could:

➤ meet in someone's home

➤ take turns meeting at different homes

➤ arrange to use a meeting room that belongs to a local community group or business

➤ meet in a local community centre, school, or church

During the second half of each journey you go out together with one or more fellow travellers to explore your community. You might:

➤ explore the outdoors by hiking, walking, bird watching, boating, going to a viewpoint, or visiting a park

➤ do creative activities such as art, cooking, drama, or crafts

➤ visit places such as museums, art galleries, club meetings, schools, or someone's home

➤ attend community events such as movies, festivals, performances, meetings, or sports

➤ get exercise by going swimming, dancing, skating, or working out

➤ socialize at places where you can play pool, darts, or board games

➤ drop in on or join other groups such as community recreation courses, clubs, or continuing education courses

➤ _____

➤ _____

➤ _____

The possibilities for where to go and what to do vary as widely as the different interests and ideas of you and the people you have connected with.

My thoughts...

Building Bridges
Box 156, Duncan, British Columbia, CANADA V9L 3X3
Phone or fax toll free: 1-888-746-1529 TTY: 1-250-746-1539

Transportation

Some people face transportation barriers such as:

My thoughts...

....
....
....
....
....
....
....
....
....
....
....
....
....
....
....
....
....
....
....
....
....
....
....

- ➤ not having a driver's license
- ➤ not having a car
- ➤ not having money for the bus
- ➤ fear of travelling alone
- ➤ difficulty getting to the bus stop
- ➤ public transportation that is not accessible
- ➤ infrequent bus schedules
- ➤ no public transportation in certain areas

If you can creatively get past these transportation barriers, you will be well on your way to discovering strong community connections. Ways of getting past transportation barriers include:

- ➤ car pooling
- ➤ taking the bus together
- ➤ walking together
- ➤ getting help from people you live with
- ➤ getting help from support workers
- ➤ using transportation services for people with disabilities
- ➤ _____
- ➤ _____
- ➤ _____

©1998 Linda D. Hill
Please obtain permission from the publisher to copy any page.
Building Bridges
Box 156, Duncan, British Columbia, CANADA V9L 3X3
Phone or fax toll free: 1-888-746-1529 TTY: 1-250-746-1539

BUILDING
BRIDGES

Journal Page

Here is a page for you to write down your plans for getting together. People usually find it easier to stick to commitments that are written down.

My thoughts...

Idea Starters

Who will be getting together?

Where will you be getting together?

When will you be getting together?

How will you each get there?

Section 3:

Journeys Of Discovery

*"We stopped off at the supermarket first, to pick up some
groceries for making butter tarts. When we got to my
place, we started to organize the ingredients and prepare.
Cindy did the pastry and I did the filling. We worked and
talked about a variety of things. She told me about her
seven year old son who is her pride and joy, and I talked
about my fiancé Ken. Our relationship grew quickly.
From the first day, a trust grew between us.
As we got to know each other we shared more."*

— Cheryl, 1989

Building Bridges
Box 156, Duncan, British Columbia, CANADA V9L 3X3
Phone or fax toll free: **1-888-746-1529** TTY: **1-250-746-1539**

Your Travel Itinerary

Now that you have found some people to travel with, packed your bags, and made a commitment to meet together, you are ready to embark on a voyage of discovery. In each of the ten journeys in this section you will find:

My thoughts...

. . . .
. . . .
. . . .
. . . .
. . . .
. . . .
. . . .
. . . .
. . . .
. . . .
. . . .
. . . .
. . . .
. . . .
. . . .
. . . .
. . . .
. . . .
. . . .
. . . .
. . . .
. . . .
. . . .

➤ a list of goals to help you know where you are going

➤ connecting skills to make the journey easier and more enjoyable

➤ a creative armchair travelling activity to get you exploring the fun of bridging disability differences

Community Connection Idea

➤ a community connection idea to encourage you to go out in your community and have fun together

➤ a journal page for you to reflect about what you are learning from each other and from this book

Within this itinerary there is complete freedom to set your own pace, choose your own route, and do what you want as you make new discoveries about yourselves, each other, and your communities.

Building Bridges
Box 156, Duncan, British Columbia, CANADA V9L 3X3
Phone or fax toll free: 1-888-746-1529 TTY: 1-250-746-1539

Skills For Connecting Across Differences

Throughout our lives there is always more to learn about how to connect with others. The more skilled each of us are at including others and being included ourselves, the easier it is to reach across our differences and get to know each other.

Here are twenty skills that make it easier to connect with each other. These skills are easy to learn by reading about what to do, watching others, practicing, and by getting feedback from people you trust. Some or many of these skills may seem easy and familiar to you. If so, then you have resources you can share with others who are at a different stage of social learning. If some of these skills seem difficult and new, then you can learn from these resource people. Everyone has resources to share and everyone has more to learn. Each connecting skill is described in Section 4, pages 73 to 93.

Check off the skills that you could help someone else practice, as well as the skills you want to learn more about.

My thoughts...

I CAN HELP SOMEONE ELSE DO THIS ✔	I WANT TO LEARN MORE ABOUT THIS ✔	
☐	☐	1. Relaxing *(page 74)*
☐	☐	2. Considering each other's needs *(page 75)*
☐	☐	3. Making small talk *(page 76)*
☐	☐	4. Taking turns talking *(page 77)*
☐	☐	5. Joining in *(page 78)*
☐	☐	6. Supporting others to participate *(page 79)*
☐	☐	7. Identifying supportive people *(page 80)*
☐	☐	8. Giving mutual support *(page 81)*
☐	☐	9. Accepting your own differences *(page 82)*
☐	☐	10. Understanding each other's differences *(page 83)*
☐	☐	11. Expressing positive feelings *(page 84)*
☐	☐	12. Listening to stories *(page 85)*
☐	☐	13. Travelling in the same direction *(page 86)*
☐	☐	14. Getting back on course *(page 87)*
☐	☐	15. Asserting your access rights *(page 88)*
☐	☐	16. Solving problems *(page 89)*
☐	☐	17. Talking positively about yourself *(page 90)*
☐	☐	18. Asking open questions *(page 91)*
☐	☐	19. Giving positive feedback *(page 92)*
☐	☐	20. Accepting positive feedback *(page 93)*

Building Bridges
Box 156, Duncan, British Columbia, CANADA V9L 3X3
Phone or fax toll free: 1-888-746-1529 TTY: 1-250-746-1539

JOURNEY ONE:

Getting Oriented

The goals for this first journey are to:

➤ get to know each other

➤ relax together

➤ help each other feel safe, share, make choices, and have fun

My thoughts...

....
....
....
....
....
....
....
....
....
....
....
....
....
....
....
....
....
....
....
....
....
....
....
....
....

> *"Meeting new people was a new experience for me. At first it was uncomfortable and I didn't know how to express myself, but I learned that barriers don't have to get in your way. That was a good thing and I think it was important. It was fun and gave me ideas to have fun and see that I could put fun into my life everyday. I feel less shy now than I did before."*   (Sarb, 1989)

Before you set out on this journey you should each be familiar with the skills of relaxing and considering each other's needs. Step by step information about these skills can be found in Section 4 on pages 74 and 75.

Armchair Travelling Activity: Double Drawing

I n double drawing, two of you hold on to the same drawing tool at the same time. Then you both draw or paint a picture together. The process of choosing colours, deciding what to draw, and enjoying the results provides on-going opportunities to practice relaxing, and supporting each other to feel safe, share, choose, and have fun.

You can change colours and add to your picture until you each feel satisfied with your joint creation. When both of you have finished your picture, hold on to a pen together and sign your names to your artwork.

You might want to try this exercise again with a different partner, different art materials, and different rules about whether or not you are allowed to talk as you draw. You might want to try triple or quadruple drawing.

My thoughts...

©1998 Linda D. Hill
Please obtain permission from the publisher to copy any page.
Building Bridges
Box 156, Duncan, British Columbia, CANADA V9L 3X3
Phone or fax toll free: 1-888-746-1529 TTY: 1-250-746-1539

BUILDING BRIDGES

*Community
Connection
Idea*

Community Connection Idea: Getting To Know Each Other

We hope each of you will get together with a couple of other people in your group and take some time to get to know each other before you go on to the next journey. Choose something to do that is safe and comfortable for each of you. A few ideas are:

➤ going for a walk together

➤ meeting at a coffee shop

➤ visiting each other in a safe and comfortable setting

➤ _____

➤ _____

➤ _____

Some people need support to keep appointments. How will you make sure that you are each able to show up at the place you've decided to meet?

When you get together, what are some ways to show consideration for each other's needs to feel safe, share, make choices, and have fun? What kind of support do each of you need from each other?

My thoughts...

....
....
....
....
....
....
....
....
....
....
....
....
....
....
....
....
....
....
....
....
....
....

©1998 Linda D. Hill
Please obtain permission from the publisher to copy any page.
Building Bridges
Box 156, Duncan, British Columbia, CANADA V9L 3X3
Phone or fax toll free: 1-888-746-1529   TTY: 1-250-746-1539

Journal Page

You can use this space to draw, write about, or paste in souvenirs about the connections you have discovered during your first journey.

My thoughts...

Idea Starters

What makes it easy and what makes it hard for you to relax, feel safe, share, make choices, and have fun?

What are your thoughts on learning from people who come from different backgrounds?

What can you do to connect with others at safe, fun and comfortable levels?

©1998 Linda D. Hill
Please obtain permission from the publisher to copy any page.
Building Bridges
Box 156, Duncan, British Columbia, CANADA V9L 3X3
Phone or fax toll free: 1-888-746-1529 TTY: 1-250-746-1539

BUILDING BRIDGES

JOURNEY TWO:

Including Fun In Our Lives

The goals for this second journey are to:

➤ have enjoyable conversations

➤ share equally in discussions

➤ explore the many ways to include fun in your lives

➤ talk about activities that are safe, fun, and free

My thoughts...

....
....
....
....
....
....
....
....
....
....
....
....
....
....
....
....
....
....
....
....
....
....
....
....

"*I was a girl who did not have many friends and I did not have enough to do so I went into this group to rebuild fun into my life. I went to coffee, roller skating, swimming, ice skating, and also five-pin bowling, and I did a lot of talking to people who were nice to me. It is a very good memory. Then I took a course called peer support. It was fun doing it for a long time and I even got a boyfriend out of the whole thing. He makes me laugh and we have a great time going on long bike rides and even on trips. We took a course together called work-search and I also took courses about early childhood education and American Sign Language and I joined the Intercultural Society. There's still more courses coming up and now I'm feeling swamped!*" (Debbie, 1994)

Before you set out on this journey you should each be familiar with the skills of making small talk and taking turns talking. Step by step information about these skills can be found in Section 4 on pages 76 and 77.

What Leisure Activities Do You Want to Explore?

To get you started, here is a questionnaire about enjoyable things you would like to get around to doing some day. List your ideas here…

	I have tried this before and liked it. ✔	I do this now and want to help others enjoy it. ✔	I have never tried this, but would like to. ✔
ACTIVITIES TO GET ME MOVING: *…like sports, exercise, dance, outdoors activities, gardening*			
______________________	☐	☐	☐
______________________	☐	☐	☐
ACTIVITIES TO GET ME CREATING AND LEARNING: *…like hobbies, arts and crafts, cooking, music, collections, adult education, computers*			
______________________	☐	☐	☐
______________________	☐	☐	☐
GAMES TO PLAY OR TO WATCH: *…like cards, board games, TV sports, lawn games*			
______________________	☐	☐	☐
______________________	☐	☐	☐
ACTIVITIES THAT INVOLVE GOING PLACES: *…like sports, concerts, libraries, museums, visiting, travelling, clubs*			
______________________	☐	☐	☐
______________________	☐	☐	☐
ACTIVITIES THAT GET ME HELPING OTHERS: *…like volunteer work, helping friends and family, visiting people who are alone*			
______________________	☐	☐	☐
______________________	☐	☐	☐

My thoughts…

Building Bridges
Box 156, Duncan, British Columbia, CANADA V9L 3X3
Phone or fax toll free: 1-888-746-1529 TTY: 1-250-746-1539

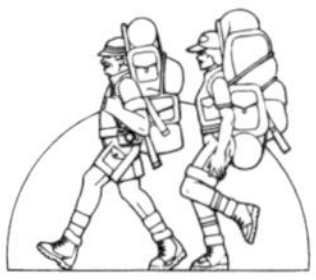

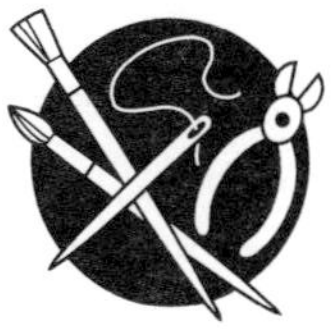

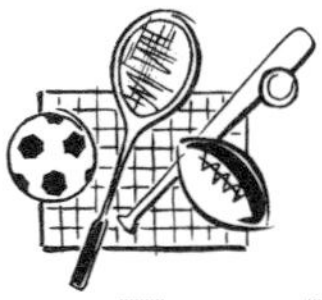

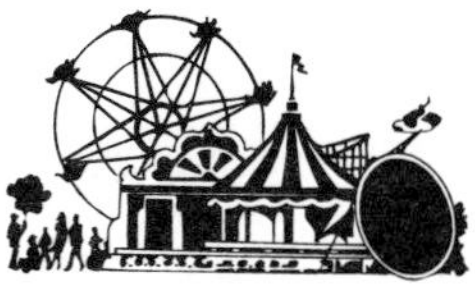

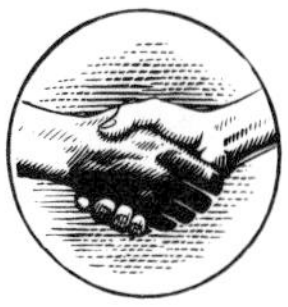

Armchair Travelling Activity: Fun. Fun? Fun!

Creatively discuss ways of including fun in your lives. Relax and open your imaginations as you explore ways to have fun that also meet your other needs to feel safe, share, and make choices.

You could make a list of the fun activities that you come up with or you could come up with a creative way of recording your ideas about having fun. Some ideas are:

➤ look through photo albums, magazines, or picture dictionaries

➤ draw pictures

➤ paint a mural

➤ cut out pictures and make a collage

➤ compose a poem about fun

➤ build a fun sculpture

➤ improvise a skit about fun

➤ put your ideas to music

➤ create a rock video

➤ _____

➤ _____

➤ _____

My thoughts...

....
....
....
....
....
....
....
....
....
....
....
....
....
....
....
....
....
....
....
....
....
....
....
....
....

Community Connection Idea:
The Best Things In Life Are Free

Community Connection Idea

Often the first ideas that pop into our heads when we look around for fun things to do are activities that cost money like: skiing, playing video games, bowling, driving go-carts, eating in restaurants, or shopping. These kinds of activities are not accessible for people who don't have a lot of money. Take a look around your community for enjoyable things to do that are free. You could go for a walk, take buses, or if someone has a car you could drive to one or more of these community resources.

➤ tourist office

➤ community centre

➤ community bulletin board

➤ municipal hall

➤ parks and recreation office

➤ library

➤ community college or another place where people go to learn things

➤ local newspaper office or another place that has a calendar of upcoming events

➤ _____

➤ _____

➤ _____

Keep notes and collect brochures about free or inexpensive things to do in your community that you might want to try.

My thoughts...

©1998 Linda D. Hill
Please obtain permission from the publisher to copy any page.
Building Bridges
Box 156, Duncan, British Columbia, CANADA V9L 3X3
Phone or fax toll free: 1-888-746-1529 TTY: 1-250-746-1539

BUILDING BRIDGES

Discovering Connections in action
— *illustrations by*
David & Faye Wetherow

Journal Page

You can use this space to draw pictures of, write about, or paste in souvenirs
of the connections you have discovered during your second journey.

My thoughts...

Idea Starters

There is an old
saying that:
"The best things
in life are free."
What are your
thoughts about
finding
enjoyable things
to do that
are free?

Some people say
that having fun
is as good a
reason to get up
in the morning
as going to work.
What are your
thoughts about
reasons for
getting up in
the morning?

©1998 Linda D. Hill
Please obtain permission from the publisher to copy any page.
Building Bridges
Box 156, Duncan, British Columbia, CANADA V9L 3X3
Phone or fax toll free: 1-888-746-1529 TTY: 1-250-746-1539

BUILDING
BRIDGES

JOURNEY THREE:
Exploring Participation And Access

The goals for this third journey are to:

➤ support each other to participate actively and equally

➤ explore access in your community

My thoughts...
....
....
....
....
....
....
....
....
....
....
....
....
....
....
....
....
....
....
....
....
....
....
....
....
....
....

"I'm extremely active in that I ride my bicycle everywhere, I swim three times a week, I attend school, and I have a part time job. But in all these things I stick pretty much to myself. Going out and doing fun things with another person is a new experience for me."

(Bernie, 1989)

Before you set out on this journey you should each be familiar with the skills of joining in and supporting each other to participate. Step by step information about these skills can be found in Section 4 on pages 78 and 79.

©1998 Linda D. Hill
Please obtain permission from the publisher to copy any page.
Building Bridges
Box 156, Duncan, British Columbia, CANADA V9L 3X3
Phone or fax toll free: 1-888-746-1529 TTY: 1-250-746-1539

JOURNEY THREE

Armchair Travelling Activity:
Mapping Your Community

Armchair Travelling

Maps give directions and show us places to go. Maps help us to see the big picture, and give information about special areas. The purpose of this mapping exercise is to help you look at the accessibility of places in your community while practicing the skills of joining in and supporting others to participate.

Together, make a map of your community. You can map your community from memory, you can get a map of your local area to draw on, you can draw a diagram, or you can make up your own way of creating a map.

Take turns thinking of places in your community that you like to go to or that you would like to go to if you could. Show these places on your map. Think about many different kinds of places such as:

➤ indoor or outdoor places

➤ viewpoints

➤ places people gather and places people like to be alone

➤ cultural places

➤ formal or informal places

➤ public or private places

➤ famous or little known places

➤ places where you live, learn, work, and play

➤ _____

➤ _____

➤ _____

Highlight your favourite places. Discuss which places are welcoming and inclusive.

My thoughts...

....
....
....
....
....
....
....
....
....
....
....
....
....
....
....
....
....
....
....
....
....
....
....
....
....
....

Community Connection Idea

Community Connection Idea: Freedom Of Choice

Look over notes from your discussions, the information you collected during your community tour, and your community map. Find accessible places to go and things to do that match with people's interests and go out to these places with two or more people.

My thoughts...

....
....
....
....
....
....
....
....
....
....
....
....
....
....
....
....
....
....
....
....
....
....
....
....
....
....

The Library is a place where we go back as kids to learn to share to listen always be there

Discovering Connections in action

— illustration by Ariane Templeton

BUILDING BRIDGES

Building Bridges
Box 156, Duncan, British Columbia, CANADA V9L 3X3
Phone or fax toll free: 1-888-746-1529 TTY: 1-250-746-1539

Journal Page

Here is more space to draw pictures of, write about, or paste in souvenirs of
the connections you have discovered during your third journey.

My thoughts . . .

Idea Starters

*What makes it
easy and what
makes it
difficult to
join in and
participate in
activities?*

*Think about
places in your
community that
are welcoming.
What makes
these places so
accessible?*

©1998 Linda D. Hill
Please obtain permission from the publisher to copy any page.
Building Bridges
Box 156, Duncan, British Columbia, CANADA V9L 3X3
Phone or fax toll free: 1-888-746-1529 TTY: 1-250-746-1539

BUILDING
BRIDGES

JOURNEY FOUR:
Exploring Interdependence

The goals for this fourth journey are to:

➤ identify supportive people

➤ explore mutual support

➤ get to know people in each other's support networks

My thoughts...

....
....
....
....
....
....
....
....
....
....
....
....
....
....
....
....
....
....
....
....
....
....
....
....

> "*When we went out together it was great because I got to get out with people I normally wouldn't have even met.*"   (Susan, 1995)
>
> "*Yeah, now I run into people I know all the time.*"   (Bob, 1995)

Before you set out on this journey you should each be familiar with the skills of identifying supportive people and giving mutual support. Step by step information about these skills can be found in Section 4 on pages 80 and 81.

BUILDING BRIDGES

©1998 Linda D. Hill
Please obtain permission from the publisher to copy any page.
Building Bridges
Box 156, Duncan, British Columbia, CANADA V9L 3X3
Phone or fax toll free: 1-888-746-1529 TTY: 1-250-746-1539

Armchair Travelling Activity:
Mapping Your Support Networks

Armchair Travelling

In the last journey you made a map of accessible places. This is an opportunity to make a map of accessible people.

There are many ways of making maps of the important people in your lives. You can draw your map; you could make a collage of photographs; you could make a diagram; or you might want to use clay, blocks, or tinker toys to represent the various people in your lives. You can also use drama to create scenes that show the important people in your lives.

Starting with yourselves, show each person in your group and show how each of you are connected to each other. Then take turns thinking of other people you are connected with and other groups you are involved in. Include the people you support as well as the people who support you. Think of:

>> family

>> friends

>> people you know from school, home, clubs, work, church, sports, and other activities

>> service providers

>> _____

>> _____

>> _____

Discuss how you support each other to feel safe, share, make choices, and have fun.

My thoughts...

©1998 Linda D. Hill
Please obtain permission from the publisher to copy any page.
Building Bridges
Box 156, Duncan, British Columbia, CANADA V9L 3X3
Phone or fax toll free: 1-888-746-1529 TTY: 1-250-746-1539

BUILDING
BRIDGES

**Community
Connection
Idea**

Community Connection Idea:
Reaching Out To Include Others

Explore ways to meet people from each other's support networks.
Two or more of you could:

> ➤ visit someone together

> ➤ invite someone to visit you

> ➤ invite someone to go out somewhere together

> ➤ invite someone to do something fun together

> ➤ invite someone to join you at your next meeting

> ➤ _____

> ➤ _____

> ➤ _____

Building healthy and supportive connections between people builds strong
and healthy communities.

My thoughts...

....
....
....
....
....
....
....
....
....
....
....
....
....
....
....
....
....
....
....
....
....
....
....
....
....

Discovering Connections in action
— illustration by
Ariane Templeton

**BUILDING
BRIDGES**

Building Bridges
Box 156, Duncan, British Columbia, CANADA V9L 3X3
Phone or fax toll free: 1-888-746-1529 TTY: 1-250-746-1539

Journal Page

You can use this space to draw pictures of, write about, or paste in souvenirs
about the connections you are discovering with important people in your life
during your fourth journey.

My thoughts...

Idea Starters

Who are the
supportive people
in your life?

What are your
support skills?

What support
do you need
from others?

What are you
learning about
mutual support?

©1998 Linda D. Hill
Please obtain permission from the publisher to copy any page.
Building Bridges
Box 156, Duncan, British Columbia, CANADA V9L 3X3
Phone or fax toll free: 1-888-746-1529 TTY: 1-250-746-1539

BUILDING
BRIDGES

JOURNEY FIVE:

Celebrating Diversity

The goals for this fifth journey are to:

> ➢ explore all types of differences, including disability differences

> ➢ enjoy learning about each other's differences

> ➢ build pride in your differences

My thoughts...

. . . .
. . . .
. . . .
. . . .
. . . .
. . . .
. . . .
. . . .
. . . .
. . . .
. . . .
. . . .
. . . .
. . . .
. . . .
. . . .
. . . .
. . . .
. . . .
. . . .

> *"I think about celebrating differences and recognizing that we all bring our own differences to the table. My dream is to be able to bring all our differences together and realize that we can make some really beautiful things happen that you couldn't otherwise do."*
>
> (Tammy, 1997)

Before you set out on this journey you should each be familiar with the skills of accepting your own differences and understanding each other's differences. Step by step information about these skills can be found in Section 4 on pages 82 and 83.

Armchair Travelling Activity: Diversity Portraits

Create portraits of each other that show each person's unique gifts, talents, special qualities, and differences that make the world a more interesting place. There are many ways of creating portraits. You could:

➤ cut out magazine pictures and photocopies of photographs to make a collage

➤ video mini documentaries about each person

➤ draw cartoons

➤ use clay, plasticine, or paper maché to create sculptures

➤ make masks

➤ write biographies or newspaper articles

➤ make computer drawings

➤ use a slide projector to project your shadows on the wall and trace them

➤ take turns standing or sitting against paper taped to a wall and trace around your profiles

➤ take photographs

➤ act out each other's life stories

➤ _____

➤ _____

➤ _____

After you finish making portraits you can discuss or write down more details about each person's diverse gifts.

My thoughts...

. . . .
. . . .
. . . .
. . . .
. . . .
. . . .
. . . .
. . . .
. . . .
. . . .
. . . .
. . . .
. . . .
. . . .
. . . .
. . . .
. . . .
. . . .
. . . .
. . . .
. . . .
. . . .
. . . .

©1998 Linda D. Hill
Please obtain permission from the publisher to copy any page.
Building Bridges
Box 156, Duncan, British Columbia, CANADA V9L 3X3
Phone or fax toll free: 1-888-746-1529 TTY: 1-250-746-1539

Art That Makes A Difference

There are many books, songs, poems, plays, movies, or other works of art that creatively deal with diversity. Here is one of our favourite poems. You may want to share your favourites with each other.

My thoughts...

When we plant a rose seed in the earth,
we notice that it is small,
but we do not criticize it as "rootless and stemless".

We treat it as a seed,
giving it the water and nourishment required of a seed.

When it first shoots up out of the earth,
we don't condemn it as immature and underdeveloped;
nor do we criticize the buds
for not being open when they appear.

We stand in wonder at the process taking place
and give the plant the care it needs
at each stage of its development.

The rose is a rose
from the time it is a seed to the time it dies.

Within it, at all times
it contains the whole process of changes;

yet at each state,
at each moment,
it is perfectly all right as it is.

(author unknown)

BUILDING BRIDGES
Building Bridges
Box 156, Duncan, British Columbia, CANADA V9L 3X3
Phone or fax toll free: 1-888-746-1529 TTY: 1-250-746-1539

Community Connection Idea:
And Now For Something Completely Different

Community Connection Idea

Think about all the differences you have shared with each other. Select one or more differences that you want to know more about. This could be:

➤ a disability difference

➤ a hobby

➤ a sport

➤ a special talent, skill, or interest

➤ a cultural or ethnic difference

➤ a unique group one of you belongs to

➤ or another type of difference

Go together with at least one other person to explore a place in the community that is connected with this difference. You could:

➤ visit a place

➤ attend a special event

➤ watch a demonstration

➤ go on a tour

➤ interview someone

➤ try an activity

➤ go to a meeting

➤ go to the library to gather information about this difference

Have fun trying out some things that are completely new and different.

My thoughts...

....
....
....
....
....
....
....
....
....
....
....
....
....
....
....
....
....
....
....
....
....

©1998 Linda D. Hill
Please obtain permission from the publisher to copy any page.
Building Bridges
Box 156, Duncan, British Columbia, CANADA V9L 3X3
Phone or fax toll free: 1-888-746-1529 TTY: 1-250-746-1539

BUILDING BRIDGES

WHEN WE MEET EACH OTHER, IT'S WITH EXCITEMENT, CURIOSITY

"A TICKET"

EXPERIENCE, TOUCH, TASTE ALL DIFFERENT CULTURES LANGUAGE

Discovering Connections in action

— illustrations by
David & Faye Wetherow

BUILDING
BRIDGES

Building Bridges
Box 156, Duncan, British Columbia, CANADA V9L 3X3
Phone or fax toll free: 1-888-746-1529 TTY: 1-250-746-1539

Journal Page

Here is some more space for you to record your reflections about connections you have discovered during your fifth journey. You may want to draw pictures, take notes, or bring back brochures about what you are learning.

My thoughts...

Idea Starters

What did you learn about disability differences and other kinds of differences from each other?

What helps people to relax about differences?

What helps people to build pride about differences?

©1998 Linda D. Hill
Please obtain permission from the publisher to copy any page.
Building Bridges
Box 156, Duncan, British Columbia, CANADA V9L 3X3
Phone or fax toll free: 1-888-746-1529 TTY: 1-250-746-1539

BUILDING
BRIDGES

JOURNEY SIX:

Feeling Good

The goals for this sixth journey are to:

> ➤ explore positive feelings

> ➤ listen to each other's stories

My thoughts...

....
....
....
....
....
....
....
....
....
....
....
....
....
....
....
....
....
....
....
....
....
....
....
....
....
....
....

> "I'm someone who is not quite positive towards myself and getting together with people makes me see the need to be more positive."
>
> (Ben, 1990)

Before you set out on this journey you should each be familiar with the skills of expressing positive feelings and listening to stories. Step by step information about these skills can be found in Section 4 on pages 84 and 85.

Armchair Travelling Activity: Remember When?

Here is a list of happy feelings:

relaxed
laid back
at peace
a sense of wonder
joyous
excited
eager
content
satisfied
pleased
interested
creative
willing
proud
free
at ease
confident
ecstatic
curious
meditative
optimistic
alert
pleasantly surprised
thoughtful
enjoying the challenge

My thoughts...

....
....
....
....
....
....
....
....
....
....
....
....
....
....
....
....
....
....
....
....
....

Think about times you have felt these feelings and share your stories with each other. You could tell stories about:

➤ happy memories about good times in your life

➤ how you solved a problem or navigated past an access barrier in your life

➤ dreams and ideas about things you would like to do or the way you would like the world to be

People commonly tell stories by sitting around talking. You can also tell stories through singing, art, drama, jokes, drawing, miming, writing, and many other ways.

©1998 Linda D. Hill
Please obtain permission from the publisher to copy any page.
Building Bridges
Box 156, Duncan, British Columbia, CANADA V9L 3X3
Phone or fax toll free: 1-888-746-1529 TTY: 1-250-746-1539

BUILDING
BRIDGES

*Community
Connection
Idea*

Community Connection Idea: Why Not?

Telling our stories and sharing our dreams are great ways to explore our connections. As you exchange ideas, experiences, and points of view you may come to a place where you find yourself saying "Why not do that again?" or "Why not try it?"

Here is an invitation to answer one of these "Why not?" questions with positive action.

My thoughts...

....
....
....
....
....
....
....
....
....
....
....
....
....
....
....
....
....
....
....
....
....
....
....

With your focus on supporting each other and daring to be different you may find something you used to enjoy that you thought was lost. You may have found a connection that you didn't realize was there before. You might:

> go back to visit a favourite place

> try a sport you have always wanted to try

> get in touch with someone you have been wanting to contact

> get together to cook a special recipe

> go and do something you have been meaning to get around to doing

> drop in on a community recreation class that you have been thinking of signing up for

> go to a meeting of a club you have been wanting to join

> get started on a project that you have been planning

> get back to a hobby or craft that you used to enjoy

> visit a place you have never been before

> _____

> _____

> _____

Why Not?

Journal Page

You can use this space to draw pictures of, write about, or paste in souvenirs
of the connections you have discovered during your sixth journey.

My thoughts...

Idea Starters

How does it feel to focus on positive feelings instead of problems?

How does it feel to listen to people who communicate in ways that are different from what you are used to?

What needs to happen for our dreams about community involvement to become reality?

©1998 Linda D. Hill
Please obtain permission from the publisher to copy any page.
Building Bridges
Box 156, Duncan, British Columbia, CANADA V9L 3X3
Phone or fax toll free: 1-888-746-1529 TTY: 1-250-746-1539

BUILDING BRIDGES

JOURNEY SEVEN:
Staying On Course

The goals of this seventh journey are to explore ways of:

➤ co-operating toward the same goals

➤ talking about the same topic

➤ supporting people to get back on course

My thoughts...

....
....
....
....
....
....
....
....
....
....
....
....
....
....
....
....
....
....
....
....
....
....
....
....

"Gary used to sit at home all day long watching television. Mostly he just sat there with the set turned off. Now he goes out with an acquaintance from the group to play tennis once a week, and he is even starting to ride his bicycle again and get out and go places on his own." (Gary's brother, 1989)

Before you set out on this journey you should each be familiar with the skills of travelling in the same direction and getting back on course. Step by step information about these skills can be found in Section 4 on pages 86 and 87.

Armchair Travelling Activity: Tower Building

Armchair Travelling

Practice travelling in the same direction and getting back on course by building a tower together. Your goal is to build a tower that is as high and as strong as possible. Your tower should be able to stand up itself without falling down. You can use:

> a building set such as Tinker Toys, Lego, or Mechano

> scrap materials such as plastic pop bottles, tape, pipe-cleaners, straws, scissors, and glue

> sculpturing materials

> building materials

> _____

> _____

> _____

There is no time limit. You might only spend a few minutes building something or you might enjoy yourselves for over an hour. The main idea is to have fun while you travel together toward the same goal of building a tall tower.

You may want to leave your tower there for others to look at or you may want to take a photograph or draw a picture of what you built before you take it down.

My thoughts...

©1998 Linda D. Hill
Please obtain permission from the publisher to copy any page.
Building Bridges
Box 156, Duncan, British Columbia, CANADA V9L 3X3
Phone or fax toll free: 1-888-746-1529 TTY: 1-250-746-1539

BUILDING BRIDGES

**Community
Connection
Idea**

Community Connection Idea: Let's Go!

Staying on course through all the steps of making new connections in the community can be a real challenge. (Perhaps it is not surprising that — without support — many of us detour to the safety of our television sets instead of getting out and getting involved).

This is an invitation to find one or more activities that are new to everyone or almost everyone, and then follow through on a plan to go out and try these activities. You can look back at:

➤ your ideas, notes, and brochures about fun from Journey Two

➤ the community map from Journey Three

➤ other ideas you have come up with during your journeys together

As you try to meet this challenge you will be practicing all the skills involved in staying on course and getting back on course. Have fun getting involved in a new activity.

My thoughts...

. . . .
. . . .
. . . .
. . . .
. . . .
. . . .
. . . .
. . . .
. . . .
. . . .
. . . .
. . . .
. . . .
. . . .
. . . .
. . . .
. . . .
. . . .
. . . .
. . . .
. . . .
. . . .
. . . .
. . . .

Discovering Connections in action

— *illustrations by
David & Faye Wetherow*

©1998 Linda D. Hill
Please obtain permission from the publisher to copy any page.
Building Bridges
Box 156, Duncan, British Columbia, CANADA V9L 3X3
Phone or fax toll free: 1-888-746-1529 TTY: 1-250-746-1539

BUILDING
BRIDGES

Journal Page

You can use this space to draw pictures of, write about, or paste in souvenirs
of the connections you have discovered during your seventh journey.

My thoughts...

Idea Starters

What kinds of things are each of you doing to help keep on a course that is safe and fun as you explore discovering connections?

What is the difference between staying on course by excluding and staying on course by including?

Building Bridges
Box 156, Duncan, British Columbia, CANADA V9L 3X3
Phone or fax toll free: 1-888-746-1529 TTY: 1-250-746-1539

BUILDING
BRIDGES

JOURNEY EIGHT:
Getting Past Access Barriers

The goals of this eighth journey are to:

➤ identify access barriers

➤ explore ways of getting past access barriers

➤ access a community recreation activity

My thoughts...

....
....
....
....
....
....
....
....
....
....
....
....
....
....
....
....
....
....
....
....
....
....
....
....
....

> *"I remember a few years ago, a group of us went out dancing and we got into a big argument with the manager who wanted us to leave because a couple of us were in wheelchairs. He said that we made the other customers feel depressed. Asking us to leave would be unthinkable today, so to me this means we've made some progress in improving community access."*   (Richard, 1985)

Before you set out on this journey you should each be familiar with the skills of asserting your access rights and solving problems. Step by step information about these skills can be found in Section 4 on pages 88 and 89.

Armchair Travelling Activity:
Exploring Ways Of Getting Past Barriers

Sometimes there are barriers that must be resolved before an individual can participate equally and actively in the community. The purpose of this activity is to practice asserting your access rights and using your problem solving skills.

1. Discuss something fun that one of you is really interested in doing.

2. Explore the main barriers that need to be solved to be able to participate equally and actively in that activity.

3. Take turns brainstorming ways to get past these access barriers.

4. Make up a skit with a happy ending that shows the best ideas for getting past these access barriers.

My thoughts...

BUILDING BRIDGES

Community Connection Idea

Community Connection Idea: Accessing Community Recreation

If it is practical, you could make the happy ending to the skit come true by going out together to do the fun activity in real life.

— *or* —

You could do some community research into resolving financial barriers:

My thoughts...

....
....
....
....
....
....
....
....
....
....
....
....
....
....
....
....
....
....
....
....
....
....
....
....

1. Find a fun activity that one or more of you really wants to try.

2. Do some research into how much it costs to do this activity.

3. Brainstorm ways of lowering this financial barrier at least temporarily. Some ideas are:

   ➤ reduced group rates

   ➤ free drop-in guest passes

   ➤ two-for-one passes

   ➤ a free or reduced rate during slow times

   ➤ do volunteer work in exchange for access to the activity

   ➤ borrow someone's equipment

   ➤ _____

   ➤ _____

   ➤ _____

   Any other ideas?

4. Hopefully this exploration will have a happy ending and you will gain access to a community recreation activity you have always wanted to try.

Building Bridges
Box 156, Duncan, British Columbia, CANADA V9L 3X3
Phone or fax toll free: 1-888-746-1529 TTY: 1-250-746-1539

BUILDING BRIDGES

Journal Page

Here is space for you to reflect on what you have learned and experienced during your eighth journey together. You may want to draw pictures, take notes, or bring back brochures about community access.

My thoughts . . .

Idea Starters

What did you learn about getting past access barriers?

What responsibilities go along with the rights to participate actively and equally?

©1998 Linda D. Hill
Please obtain permission from the publisher to copy any page.
Building Bridges
Box 156, Duncan, British Columbia, CANADA V9L 3X3
Phone or fax toll free: 1-888-746-1529 TTY: 1-250-746-1539

BUILDING BRIDGES

JOURNEY NINE:
Building Trust In Ourselves And Others

The goals of this ninth journey are to:

➤ explore how you are building trust in yourself

➤ explore how you are building trust in each other

My thoughts...

....
....
....
....
....
....
....
....
....
....
....
....
....
....
....
....
....
....
....
....
....
....
....
....
....
....

"We've started to accept each other, each as individuals all with differences. We are learning patience, learning to listen, and learning to include. We've learned from each other's individual backgrounds: understanding each person as a person and then developing empathy."   (Susan, 1997)

Before you set out on this journey you should each be familiar with the skills of talking positively about yourself and asking open questions. Step by step information about these skills can be found in Section 4 on pages 90 and 91.

©1998 Linda D. Hill
Please obtain permission from the publisher to copy any page.
Building Bridges
Box 156, Duncan, British Columbia, CANADA V9L 3X3
Phone or fax toll free: 1-888-746-1529 TTY: 1-250-746-1539

Armchair Travelling Activity: Open Interviews

Practice talking positively about yourself and asking open questions by interviewing each other about your life stories. Here are some types of open questions you could ask each other:

1. What are some of the interesting things you have done or places you have been in your life?

2. What are some of your interests or passions in your life?

3. What are some skills you have learned or talents you have developed in your life?

4. What are some of the ways you have helped others in your life?

5. What are some of the compliments you have received or times you have been recognized or honoured in your life?

6. What are some of the important lessons you have learned in your life that you would like to pass on to others?

There are many creative ways you could interview each other:

➤ look at old photo-albums, scrap-books, or other memorabilia together

➤ demonstrate or show off interesting things you have learned or done in your life

➤ make a television show about your life and times

➤ pretend you are a journalist writing an article for a newspaper

➤ draw, paint, or sculpture your answers to these questions

➤ _____

➤ _____

➤ _____

My thoughts...

....
....
....
....
....
....
....
....
....
....
....
....
....
....
....
....
....
....
....
....
....
....
....
....

©1998 Linda D. Hill
Please obtain permission from the publisher to copy any page.
Building Bridges
Box 156, Duncan, British Columbia, CANADA V9L 3X3
Phone or fax toll free: 1-888-746-1529 TTY: 1-250-746-1539

BUILDING
BRIDGES

Community Connection Idea: Sharing Time Together

We hope each of you will get together with at least a couple of other people in your group to share some quality time together before you set out on the last journey in this guidebook. You may want to reflect with each other on where these journeys have taken you and what you have learned from each other. Hopefully you have come a long way in building trust in yourselves and in each other.

You may want to go out and enjoy a community recreation activity together or have a good long visit together in a comfortable place.

My thoughts...

....
....
....
....
....
....
....
....
....
....
....
....
....
....
....
....
....
....
....
....
....
....
....
....
....

Discovering Connections in action
— illustration by
David & Faye Wetherow

©1998 Linda D. Hill
Please obtain permission from the publisher to copy any page.
Building Bridges
Box 156, Duncan, British Columbia, CANADA V9L 3X3
Phone or fax toll free: 1-888-746-1529 TTY: 1-250-746-1539

Journal Page

You can use this space to draw pictures of, write about or paste in souvenirs of the connections you have discovered during your ninth journey.

My thoughts...

Idea Starters

What does it mean to be your own best friend?

What are the keys to building trust with each other?

Building Bridges
Box 156, Duncan, British Columbia, CANADA V9L 3X3
Phone or fax toll free: 1-888-746-1529 TTY: 1-250-746-1539

JOURNEY TEN:
Saying Good-bye

The goals for this tenth journey are to:

➤ give positive feedback to each other

➤ plan a good-bye celebration

➤ celebrate the time you have spent *discovering connections* together

My thoughts...

. . . .
. . . .
. . . .
. . . .
. . . .
. . . .
. . . .
. . . .
. . . .
. . . .
. . . .
. . . .
. . . .
. . . .
. . . .
. . . .
. . . .
. . . .
. . . .
. . . .
. . . .

My Thanks and Tribute

Oh what a glorious morning
Oh what a glorious week
I've got a glorious feeling
This group has been a Royal treat.

We've cared and we've shared
And we've had much to declare.
We learned and extolled.
And stuck to our goals.

Much for congrats
A fun group
We party and go!

(Diane, 1996)

Before you set out on this journey you should each be familiar with the skills of giving and accepting positive feedback. Step by step information about these skills can be found in Section 4 on pages 92 and 93.

Celebrate The Connections You've Discovered!

Armchair Travelling Activity: Planning A Good-bye Celebration

Here is an invitation to plan a special event to celebrate the gifts you have been giving to each other and the connections you have made during your journeys together. Celebrations can be big or small, quiet or extravagant, here or there, or anywhere. Here are some ideas for the types of celebrations you could plan:

My thoughts...

....
....
....
....
....
....
....
....
....
....
....
....
....
....
....
....
....
....
....
....
....
....
....

➤ a party

➤ a meal

➤ going some place special

➤ doing something active together

➤ a talent show

➤ an event with speeches and certificates

➤ gift giving

➤ card making

➤ a ceremony

➤ a picnic

➤ _____

➤ _____

➤ _____

Best of luck in planning a memorable and enjoyable way of finishing up this book together.

©1998 Linda D. Hill
Please obtain permission from the publisher to copy any page.
Building Bridges
Box 156, Duncan, British Columbia, CANADA V9L 3X3
Phone or fax toll free: 1-888-746-1529 TTY: 1-250-746-1539

BUILDING BRIDGES

Community Connection Idea: Saying Good-bye

You've made your plans, so the only thing left to do is to celebrate! There is room on this page to collect autographs, addresses and phone numbers to help you keep in touch with each other.

My thoughts...

....
....
....
....
....
....
....
....
....
....
....
....
....
....
....
....
....
....
....
....
....
....
....
....

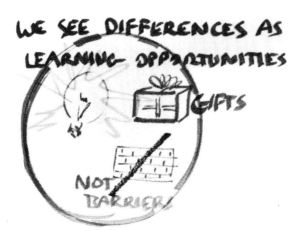

Discovering Connections in action
— *illustrations by*
David & Faye Wetherow

Journal Page: A Mirror For Your Thoughts

Think of this page as a mirror, reflecting your thoughts back to you.
Show what this book has meant in your journey through life.

My thoughts...

Idea Starters

Where were
you at the
beginning of
the book?

What lasting
learning about
discovering
connections
have you
experienced?

Where do you
plan to go
from here?

Section 4:

Connecting Skills

"Monday came and met you all
Having fun here.
Tuesday breaking down these walls
Having fun here.
Wednesday we all learned
How to line dance.
Thursday found us more relaxed
As we took a chance.
Friday came and we've had fun
Making friends here.
We will do this all again.
Let's not wait a year."

— Margie, 1996

Please obtain permission from the publisher to copy any page.

Building Bridges
Box 156, Duncan, British Columbia, CANADA V9L 3X3
Phone or fax toll free: 1-888-746-1529   TTY: 1-250-746-1539

BUILDING
BRIDGES

Skill One: Relaxing

Relaxing your body opens your mind. There are many different ways to relax. Here are some ideas to try:

1. Take one or two deep breaths.

2. Close your eyes for a moment and picture a place where you feel safe and relaxed. Some people imagine sitting in a favourite chair, looking at a view, gardening, or playing sports.

3. Talk yourself into relaxing. Tell yourself that you are safe and this will be fun.

4. It is easier to relax when you are with people you trust, so plan to stay close to someone you trust until you get to know everyone else.

5. Make a joke or laugh at someone else's joke.

6. Look around the room to notice the people and the things in the room that feel safe and relaxing.

7. Play an ice-breaker game.

8. Practice loosening your muscles:

   ➤ Sit comfortably in your chair or on the floor with your arms at your sides (uncrossed).

   ➤ Take a deep breath, hold it for a few seconds, then breathe out slowly. As you breathe out try to get your whole body to feel soft and loose from your head to your toes. Take some more deep breaths until your body feels relaxed.

   ➤ If you still feel a bit tense then stretch out your arms and legs, shrug your shoulders, and yawn. Now, sit comfortably again and take another deep breath.

   ➤ Practice relaxing for a few minutes each day. Soon you will easily be able to relax after just one breath.

> Journey One has an armchair travelling activity on page 27 that will give you an opportunity to experience and practice relaxing.

My thoughts...

....
....
....
....
....
....
....
....
....
....
....
....
....
....
....
....
....
....
....
....
....
....
....

 BUILDING BRIDGES

©1998 Linda D. Hill
Please obtain permission from the publisher to copy any page.
Building Bridges
Box 156, Duncan, British Columbia, CANADA V9L 3X3
Phone or fax toll free: 1-888-746-1529 TTY: 1-250-746-1539

Skill Two: Considering Each Other's Needs

Our basic social needs are to feel safe, contribute, make choices, and have fun. A big part of connecting with others is supporting each other in ways that these social needs are met.

1. Help each other feel physically and emotionally safe and comfortable.

2. Help each other share. Give ideas and welcome each other's contributions. Explore different ideas for ways everyone can be an active and contributing group member.

3. Help each other make choices. Listen to each other and respect people's rights to make choices that are different from what you would choose.

4. Help each other have fun. Laugh together, play together, and see the funny side of life's situations.

My thoughts...

Journey One has an armchair travelling activity on page 27 that will give you an opportunity to experience and practice considering each other's needs.

BUILDING BRIDGES

Skill Three: Making Small Talk

We make small talk for a little while with people we don't know well or when we first get together. Small talk breaks the ice and helps everyone relax and feel safe.

My thoughts...

1. Relax first and then go up to someone to start a conversation.

2. Make comments, tell jokes, or ask questions about things that are light, comfortable, and safe. Some comfortable and safe topics are:

   ➤ the situation you are both in; such as the weather, physical surroundings, the activity you are doing

   ➤ good news that you already know about each other; such as sports, family, friends, housing, work, movies, travel

   ➤ neutral topics; such as where you are from, where you grew up, where you went to school

3. Talk about positive topics. If you talk about problems at the beginning of a conversation, then people feel uncomfortable. When you talk about happy topics, then people have fun and feel safe with you.

Journey Two has an armchair travelling activity on page 32 that will give you an opportunity to experience and practice making small talk.

BUILDING BRIDGES

©1998 Linda D. Hill
Please obtain permission from the publisher to copy any page.
Building Bridges
Box 156, Duncan, British Columbia, CANADA V9L 3X3
Phone or fax toll free: 1-888-746-1529 TTY: 1-250-746-1539

Skill Four: Taking Turns Talking

In a good discussion everyone takes turns talking. This includes people who feel shy, people who talk slowly, or people who communicate in alternative ways. Here are some things you can do to help everyone take turns talking.

1. Show that you are interested.
   - ➤ lean forward
   - ➤ look at the person who is talking
   - ➤ nod and encourage

2. Take your turn and then wait so that each person gets a chance to talk.

3. Ask each other "What do you think?"

4. Give positive feedback to each other.
   - ➤ agree
   - ➤ smile
   - ➤ make encouraging comments such as "yes" or "good idea"
   - ➤ summarize the key point of what someone says, "so you mean…"

5. Listen to all kinds of talking.
   - ➤ writing
   - ➤ signing
   - ➤ alternative communication
   - ➤ body language
   - ➤ drawing
   - ➤ pointing
   - ➤ demonstrating
   - ➤ facial expression

6. Be open to finding and accepting interpreters.
   - ➤ professional interpreters for formal situations
   - ➤ fluent communicators for informal talks
   - ➤ understanding friends, family members, and support workers who know how to support communication without taking over

My thoughts…

....
....
....
....
....
....
....
....
....
....
....
....
....
....
....
....
....
....
....
....
....
....

Journey Two has an armchair travelling activity on page 32 that will give you an opportunity to experience and practice taking turns talking.

©1998 Linda D. Hill
Please obtain permission from the publisher to copy any page.
Building Bridges
Box 156, Duncan, British Columbia, CANADA V9L 3X3
Phone or fax toll free: 1-888-746-1529 TTY: 1-250-746-1539

Skill Five: Joining In

People who are willing to join in and participate in activities are fun to be with.

1. Check to make sure the activity is safe. (Remember you do not have to participate in any activities that feel unsafe or uncomfortable for you).

2. Relax and watch until you feel you understand the activity and feel ready to join in.

3. Ask questions to learn more about an activity.
   - ➤ "What is this all about?"
   - ➤ "How do you do this?"
   - ➤ "How do you play?"
   - ➤ "What do I do?"

4. Participate when you feel ready.

5. Here are some things to try if an activity feels difficult.
   - ➤ ask for help
   - ➤ take your time
   - ➤ cheer others on
   - ➤ try just part of an activity
   - ➤ find a different way of doing the activity

My thoughts...

....
....
....
....
....
....
....
....
....
....
....
....
....
....
....
....
....
....
....
....
....
....
....
....

Journey Three has an armchair travelling activity on page 37 that will give you an opportunity to experience and practice joining in.

©1998 Linda D. Hill
Please obtain permission from the publisher to copy any page.
Building Bridges
Box 156, Duncan, British Columbia, CANADA V9L 3X3
Phone or fax toll free: 1-888-746-1529   TTY: 1-250-746-1539

Skill Six: Supporting Each Other To Participate

You can help each other get involved in activities in a number of ways.

1. Get involved yourself — your participation is catching.

2. Invite people to join in with you.

3. Think of the activity as being like a jigsaw puzzle. Look for ways to take the activity apart and support each other to participate in a piece of the activity at a time.

4. Experiment with different ways that people can get involved and participate.

5. Do the activity together in pairs or small groups

6. Welcome people who begin to get involved, even if they've taken a little longer to get started or if they are approaching things a little differently.

7. Acknowledge everyone's contributions.

My thoughts...

Journey Three has an armchair travelling activity on page 37 that will give you an opportunity to experience and practice supporting each other to participate.

Building Bridges
Box 156, Duncan, British Columbia, CANADA V9L 3X3
Phone or fax toll free: 1-888-746-1529 TTY: 1-250-746-1539

BUILDING
BRIDGES

Skill Seven: Identifying Supportive People

The more time you can spend with supportive people, the better you will feel about yourself.

1. Some people are good at helping others feel good.
   These are people who know how to:
   - listen
   - encourage
   - wait and give space and time
   - understand feelings

2. Some people are good at solving problems. These people are able to:
   - clarify
   - share information
   - go step by step through a problem
   - suggest ideas
   - search for the best solution
   - help others to stand up for their rights
   - get others to listen to what you need

3. Some people are good at giving. These are people who can give:
   - time
   - money
   - transportation
   - food
   - clothing
   - gifts
   - surprises

4. Some people are good at doing. These are people who can:
   - lend a hand
   - clean up
   - fix things
   - go places
   - get things happening

Different people are good at giving different kinds of support. Each of us has different kinds of support skills. Identify what kinds of support other people give you. Identify what kinds of support you give to others.

> Journey Four has an armchair travelling activity on page 41 that will give you an opportunity to experience and practice identifying supportive people.

My thoughts...

....
....
....
....
....
....
....
....
....
....
....
....
....
....
....
....
....
....
....
....
....
....
....

BUILDING BRIDGES

©1998 Linda D. Hill
Please obtain permission from the publisher to copy any page.
Building Bridges
Box 156, Duncan, British Columbia, CANADA V9L 3X3
Phone or fax toll free: 1-888-746-1529 TTY: 1-250-746-1539

Skill Eight: Giving Mutual Support

Giving mutual support gives everyone a chance to contribute.

1. Help each other keep your relationship in balance.

    ➤ take turns phoning and visiting

    ➤ accept support as well as giving support

    ➤ help each other feel safe, share, make choices, and have fun

    ➤ exchange gifts, letters, notes of appreciation once in a while

My thoughts...

2. Keep the relationship positive.

    ➤ do things together that are fun

    ➤ share mostly good news

    ➤ laugh together

    ➤ solve problems early instead of waiting until they get big

    ➤ surprise each other in ways that are fun and not scary

3. Be open to adding new people to your support network.

    ➤ join new activities, clubs, and courses

    ➤ invite each other's friends to join you

    ➤ be careful of jealousy and exclusion

    ➤ share people

    ➤ "the more the merrier"

    ➤ "strength in numbers"

> Journey Four has an armchair travelling activity on page 41 that will give you an opportunity to experience and practice giving mutual support.

Building Bridges
Box 156, Duncan, British Columbia, CANADA V9L 3X3
Phone or fax toll free: 1-888-746-1529 TTY: 1-250-746-1539

BUILDING
BRIDGES

Skill Nine: Accepting Your Own Differences

1. Be friendly and relaxed.

2. Learn about your differences so that you can understand and accept who you are.

3. Find positive things about your unique qualities to feel good about.

4. Be willing to show or tell people what to do to help them learn about, accept, and understand your differences.

My thoughts...

. . . .
. . . .
. . . .
. . . .
. . . .
. . . .
. . . .
. . . .
. . . .
. . . .
. . . .
. . . .
. . . .
. . . .
. . . .
. . . .
. . . .
. . . .
. . . .
. . . .
. . . .
. . . .
. . . .

Journey Five has an armchair travelling activity on page 45 that will give you an opportunity to experience and practice accepting your own differences.

BUILDING BRIDGES

©1998 Linda D. Hill
Please obtain permission from the publisher to copy any page.
Building Bridges
Box 156, Duncan, British Columbia, CANADA V9L 3X3
Phone or fax toll free: 1-888-746-1529 TTY: 1-250-746-1539

Skill Ten: Understanding Each Other's Differences

1. Open your mind.
   - ➢ listen with open ears and eyes
   - ➢ look from all viewpoints
   - ➢ ask polite questions
   - ➢ show interest

2. Open your heart.
   - ➢ relax
   - ➢ be warm
   - ➢ show respect

3. Open your arms.
   - ➢ reach out and welcome
   - ➢ give a hand if needed
   - ➢ show support
   - ➢ travel together for awhile

My thoughts...

Journey Five has an armchair travelling activity on page 45 that will give you an opportunity to experience and practice understanding each other's differences.

Building Bridges
Box 156, Duncan, British Columbia, CANADA V9L 3X3
Phone or fax toll free: 1-888-746-1529   TTY: 1-250-746-1539

Skill Eleven: Expressing Positive Feelings

1. Expressing positive feelings is fun and good for our health. Notice how soft, light, and loose your body feels when you are enjoying yourself. Learn the names of the many positive feelings associated with having fun. Here is a list of some happy feelings:

My thoughts...

relaxed	proud
laid back	free
at peace	at ease
a sense of wonder	confident
joyous	ecstatic
excited	curious
eager	meditative
content	optimistic
satisfied	alert
pleased	pleasantly surprised
interested	thoughtful
creative	enjoying the challenge
willing	

2. Notice the people, places, and activities in your life that bring on these feelings and think about how you could spend more time with those people, in those places, and doing those activities.

3. Search for new people, places and activities that make you feel good so that you have lots of choices.

4. Tell stories about people, places, and activities that have helped you feel good. Your positive stories will help others feel good too.

> Journey Six has an armchair travelling activity on page 51 that will give you an opportunity to experience and practice expressing positive feelings.

©1998 Linda D. Hill
Please obtain permission from the publisher to copy any page.
Building Bridges
Box 156, Duncan, British Columbia, CANADA V9L 3X3
Phone or fax toll free: 1-888-746-1529 TTY: 1-250-746-1539

Skill Twelve: Listening To Stories

People who can listen to stories with their hearts as well as their heads are considered to be wonderful listeners and great sources of support.

1. Look interested and pay attention to what the other person is saying.

2. Be willing to accept interpreting support so that you can listen to all kinds of talking including alternative communication and sign language.

3. Encourage the person to tell you more about the topic.

4. Listen to the person's words and watch their face and body language.

5. As you listen, try to put yourself in that person's shoes to fully understand his or her point of view and feelings. Try to reflect those feelings with your face and body language.

6. Put those feelings into words and reflect them back to the person who is talking to check your understanding.

My thoughts...

....
....
....
....
....
....
....
....
....
....
....
....
....
....
....
....
....
....
....
....
....
....
....

Journey Six has an armchair travelling activity on page 51 that will give you an opportunity to experience and practice listening to stories.

©1998 Linda D. Hill
Please obtain permission from the publisher to copy any page.
Building Bridges
Box 156, Duncan, British Columbia, CANADA V9L 3X3
Phone or fax toll free: 1-888-746-1529 TTY: 1-250-746-1539

BUILDING
BRIDGES

Skill Thirteen: Travelling In The Same Direction

Talking about the same topic or co-operating toward the same goals are two ways of supporting each other to go in the same direction.

1. First, listen and figure out what the topic of the conversation is or what the goals of the activity are. If you can't figure it out then ask.

   ➤ "What is everyone talking about?"

   ➤ "What is everyone trying to do right now?"

2. Once you know what the topic is or what the goals are, you can join in:

   a. When you are talking together you can stay on topic by:

      ➤ asking questions

      ➤ answering questions

      ➤ giving ideas or information

      ➤ expressing feelings

   b. When you are doing something together you can help reach goals by:

      ➤ asking for what you need

      ➤ sharing what you have

      ➤ offering your skills and ideas

      ➤ acknowledging other's contributions

My thoughts...

....
....
....
....
....
....
....
....
....
....
....
....
....
....
....
....
....
....
....
....
....
....
....

Journey Seven has an armchair travelling activity on page 55 that will give you an opportunity to experience and practice travelling in the same direction.

©1998 Linda D. Hill
Please obtain permission from the publisher to copy any page.
Building Bridges
Box 156, Duncan, British Columbia, CANADA V9L 3X3
Phone or fax toll free: 1-888-746-1529 TTY: 1-250-746-1539

Skill Fourteen: Getting Back On Course

Sometimes people lose track of what the rest of the group is talking about or what the rest of the group is doing. Maybe they didn't hear or they didn't understand some of the words. Maybe they got distracted. Maybe they are too worried or preoccupied to easily tune in on other people's interests or goals for the moment.

You can support people to get back on course in respectful and supportive ways.

1. Listen and watch carefully.

2. Try to find ways that what the person is saying or doing connects to what the rest of the group is saying or doing.

2. Talk about or show the connections you notice to help the rest of the group understand.

3. Mention generally what the topic or goals are to help everyone get back on course.

My thoughts...

> Journey Seven has an armchair travelling activity on page 55 that will give you an opportunity to experience and practice getting back on course.

BUILDING
BRIDGES

Skill Fifteen: Asserting Your Access Rights

1. Be aware that everyone has the right to participate actively and equally in the community.

2. Be aware that there are many different kinds of barriers that stop people from full participation in their communities.
   Here are some kinds of barriers:
   - physical
   - financial
   - time
   - communication and information
   - negative attitudes
   - discrimination
   - red tape
   - isolation and loneliness
   - transportation
   - emotional difficulties
   - educational barriers

3. When you come up against a barrier, don't give up or lose your cool. Tell yourself that sooner or later you will find a way to get around that barrier to where you want to go.

4. Two heads are better than one so find a supportive person who will listen to you.

5. Find a quiet time and place to meet together.
   - stop and relax
   - think
   - discuss ideas to get past the barrier
   - select the best idea or combination of ideas

6. Follow through with an action plan.

Journey Eight has an armchair travelling activity on page 59 that will give you an opportunity to experience and practice asserting your access rights.

My thoughts...

·····················
·····················
·····················
·····················
·····················
·····················
·····················
·····················
·····················
·····················
·····················
·····················
·····················
·····················
·····················
·····················
·····················
·····················
·····················
·····················
·····················
·····················
·····················

BUILDING BRIDGES

©1998 Linda D. Hill
Please obtain permission from the publisher to copy any page.
Building Bridges
Box 156, Duncan, British Columbia, CANADA V9L 3X3
Phone or fax toll free: 1-888-746-1529 TTY: 1-250-746-1539

Skill Sixteen: Solving Problems

1. The first step is to listen. Relax to open your mind and think carefully while you are listening. Before you can help solve a problem you need to find out as much as possible about what the person is interested in doing and where the person is interested in going.

2. Clarify the barriers by asking:

   ➤ "What is stopping you?"

   ➤ "What else is stopping you from doing what you want?"

3. Take turns brainstorming as many ways as possible to get past the barrier to do what the person is interested in doing.

4. Find one or more ideas that might work.

5. Try out the action plan.

6. Check later to see if the action plan has worked.

My thoughts...

```
. . . . . . . . . . . . . . . . . . . . . . . .
. . . . . . . . . . . . . . . . . . . . . . . .
. . . . . . . . . . . . . . . . . . . . . . . .
. . . . . . . . . . . . . . . . . . . . . . . .
. . . . . . . . . . . . . . . . . . . . . . . .
. . . . . . . . . . . . . . . . . . . . . . . .
. . . . . . . . . . . . . . . . . . . . . . . .
. . . . . . . . . . . . . . . . . . . . . . . .
. . . . . . . . . . . . . . . . . . . . . . . .
. . . . . . . . . . . . . . . . . . . . . . . .
. . . . . . . . . . . . . . . . . . . . . . . .
. . . . . . . . . . . . . . . . . . . . . . . .
. . . . . . . . . . . . . . . . . . . . . . . .
. . . . . . . . . . . . . . . . . . . . . . . .
. . . . . . . . . . . . . . . . . . . . . . . .
. . . . . . . . . . . . . . . . . . . . . . . .
. . . . . . . . . . . . . . . . . . . . . . . .
. . . . . . . . . . . . . . . . . . . . . . . .
. . . . . . . . . . . . . . . . . . . . . . . .
. . . . . . . . . . . . . . . . . . . . . . . .
. . . . . . . . . . . . . . . . . . . . . . . .
. . . . . . . . . . . . . . . . . . . . . . . .
. . . . . . . . . . . . . . . . . . . . . . . .
. . . . . . . . . . . . . . . . . . . . . . . .
. . . . . . . . . . . . . . . . . . . . . . . .
. . . . . . . . . . . . . . . . . . . . . . . .
. . . . . . . . . . . . . . . . . . . . . . . .
```

Journey Eight has an armchair travelling activity on page 59 that will give you an opportunity to experience and practice solving problems.

©1998 Linda D. Hill
Please obtain permission from the publisher to copy any page.
Building Bridges
Box 156, Duncan, British Columbia, CANADA V9L 3X3
Phone or fax toll free: 1-888-746-1529   TTY: 1-250-746-1539

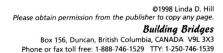

BUILDING BRIDGES

Skill Seventeen: Talking Positively About Yourself

You can build up your trust in yourself by being your own best friend.

1. Get in the habit of taking time every day to think about all the things that have gone well such as:

   ➤ people, activities, and places you have enjoyed

   ➤ ways you have helped or been helped

   ➤ special qualities you have noticed in yourself and others

   ➤ daily successes

   ➤ fun experiences

2. Talk to yourself about these positive things every day, especially before you try something new or difficult. Talk about these positive things any time that you want to build up your self confidence.

3. Talk to other people about what is going well. People like to hear good news.

My thoughts...

....
....
....
....
....
....
....
....
....
....
....
....
....
....
....
....
....
....
....
....
....
....
....
....
....

Journey Nine has an armchair travelling activity on page 63 that will give you an opportunity to experience and practice talking positively about yourself.

©1998 Linda D. Hill
Please obtain permission from the publisher to copy any page.
Building Bridges
Box 156, Duncan, British Columbia, CANADA V9L 3X3
Phone or fax toll free: 1-888-746-1529 TTY: 1-250-746-1539

Skill Eighteen: Asking Open Questions

Listening to each other is a key to building trust. Open questions can help people trust you enough to open up and share with you.

1. Ask questions that meet each other's social needs to:

   ➤ feel safe

   ➤ share

   ➤ make choices

   ➤ have fun

2. Ask questions that give people freedom to give you a long answer back. If you ask a closed question that calls for a one word answer such as "yes" or "no", then follow it up with an open question.

3. Be careful not to scare people by asking too many questions at once.

4. Wait patiently after you ask a question. Some people take longer to get started than others.

5. Remember to respect people's right to be quiet. People who feel comfortable listening to silence are often considered to be the most trusted companions of all.

My thoughts...

Journey Nine has an armchair travelling activity on page 63 that will give you an opportunity to experience and practice asking open questions.

Building Bridges
Box 156, Duncan, British Columbia, CANADA V9L 3X3
Phone or fax toll free: 1-888-746-1529   TTY: 1-250-746-1539

Skill Nineteen: Giving Positive Feedback

Giving positive feedback and sincere compliments helps people feel good about themselves and about you.

1. Notice positive things that other people do or say:

   ➢ things they are good at

   ➢ ways they help others

   ➢ things they do that make it enjoyable to be with them

   ➢ things that you would like to thank them for

2. Make short comments about what you notice directly to the person in an honest, sincere, and respectful way.

My thoughts...

. . . .
. . . .
. . . .
. . . .
. . . .
. . . .
. . . .
. . . .
. . . .
. . . .
. . . .
. . . .
. . . .
. . . .
. . . .
. . . .
. . . .
. . . .
. . . .
. . . .
. . . .
. . . .

Journey Ten has an armchair travelling activity on page 68 that will give you an opportunity to experience and practice giving positive feedback.

Skill Twenty: Accepting Positive Feedback

Guess what?

> ➤ You don't have to blush and giggle.

> ➤ You don't have to run away and hide.

> ➤ You don't have to say "No, no, no, that nice thing you said couldn't be true."

> ➤ You don't have to disagree with the nice thing someone is saying about you.

> ➤ You don't even have to figure out something nicer to say back.

If someone gives you a compliment, you can simply smile and say "thank you".

My thoughts...

. . . .
. . . .
. . . .
. . . .
. . . .
. . . .
. . . .
. . . .
. . . .
. . . .
. . . .
. . . .
. . . .
. . . .
. . . .
. . . .
. . . .
. . . .
. . . .
. . . .
. . . .
. . . .
. . . .

Journey Ten has an armchair travelling activity on page 68 that will give you an opportunity to experience and practice accepting positive feedback.

Section 5:

More Connections

"You are creating opportunities. In some ways, what **Discovering Connections** *is about is creating the opportunities for more and more people to have these experiences together. And it's easy. Somebody said, 'Everybody is laughing and it's fun and it's easy.' In some ways it's like a big stained glass window with lights behind it. What you want to do when you are doing your work together, is try to make the lights come on behind as many of these qualities as possible."*

— David Wetherow, The Community Institute, December 8, 1997

Building Bridges
Box 156, Duncan, British Columbia, CANADA V9L 3X3
Phone or fax toll free: 1-888-746-1529   TTY: 1-250-746-1539

Our Journey Toward Writing This Guidebook

by Linda Hill and Cathy La France

My thoughts...

Linda: *"For me, the journey toward writing this guidebook began about ten years ago. I had just returned from a life-changing year of cross-cultural learning in the South Pacific. My first job in Canada was working at a Community Mental Health Centre. I found myself exploring ways that people who lived in psychiatric boarding homes could decrease social isolation and increase their participation in community recreation and leisure activities. At the same time I was running integration groups in schools and community centres for kids with disabilities and their siblings, friends, and classmates. I thought that my integration approach might work with adults and so I invited community volunteers to join boarding home residents in an integrated course I called **Rebuilding Fun Into Life**. This course had a focus on exploring fun instead of analyzing problems and participants found it to be a great way of bridging isolation gaps. It felt like any cross-cultural encounter. The lines separating volunteers and boarding home residents faded as negative stereotypes, prejudices, and 'us helping them' attitudes were replaced by relaxation, interest, and enjoyment of our different life experiences. And, just as we noticed that participating in integrated groups was good for all kids, participating in **Rebuilding Fun Into Life** was good for all the adults, not just the mental health clients. Social isolation was one barrier that made it hard to get active and have fun but over-work was another big barrier. Some of us had become so busy that we had pushed fun out of our lives. The more we recognized that we each needed help to rebuild that childhood sense of fun and play back into life, the more mutually supportive the groups became. Eventually, I began offering **Rebuilding Fun Into Life** courses in other communities and in 1991 I had the good fortune to link up with the Cowichan Valley Independent Living Resource Centre."*

Cathy: *"Initially I was skeptical. Linda had said that the course was based on a theory called 'reverse integration'. Alarm bells went off for me because I feel the theory of integration has some real flaws. For instance, I believe you can become a member of a community but still not be fully accepted or included. I had also seen some professionals who, when marketing their latest research on integration, had completely exploited the individuals they were 'saving from isolation'. The concept of inclusion, however, takes things a step farther than integration. With inclusion you are offered the opportunity to be a member of a community and to fully participate in the life of that community.*

"Linda had also said that the course involved matching the participants in pairs (one person labelled with a disability and one person learning support skills) to go out together and explore fun things to do in the community, while practicing their social and support skills. For me, matching people up to explore the community did not feel like a natural or safe way to develop a social relationship. Too often, people with disabilities have had many decisions made for them, and not been given opportunities to make their own informed choices in their lives. Maintaining this kind of control over one's life is an integral part of the Independent Living Philosophy we adhere to in our organization. Also, dividing people into categories of those who want to learn how to support people with disabilities and those who have a disability that need support to learn social skills only serves to perpetuate stereotypes associated with people with disabilities. Promoting the idea of mutual learning seemed to make much more sense to me. Linda and I discussed these philosophical differences and she agreed to make some minor changes in the course.

"I have never regretted this experience and, as I said in the preface, I found myself truly having fun while we learned more about the issues related to social isolation, how to create an inclusive atmosphere with a very diverse group of people, and finally how to support each other in an empowering way."

Linda: "Since 1996 I have been discovering connections with the Island Deaf and Hard of Hearing Centre (IDHHC) in Victoria, BC. The "Sign Up For Fun" groups I do with IDHHC bring people from several different worlds together: members of the mainstream Deaf community, Deaf people with disabilities, Hard of Hearing people, and Hearing people who can sign. The inclusive process with a focus on fun and mutual learning helps participants enjoyably discover connections while exploring challenging topics such as communication diversity, Deaf/Hearing relations, and community access issues."

Cathy: "I would hope that we would eventually see differences, and what we now call disabilities, as learning opportunities rather than barriers. It is really important that we begin to see things more from a multicultural perspective where we respect differences and see them as opportunities to learn, and accept each other for who we are rather than trying to fit people into the same kind of mold."

My thoughts...

My thoughts...

....
....
....
....
....
....
....
....
....
....
....
....
....
....
....
....
....
....
....
....
....
....
....
....
....

New Paths And New Possibilities

On December 8, 1997 a diverse cross-section of about twenty people who had been on various *Discovering Connections* journeys got together. Many of us were meeting each other for the first time. With the help of **David** and **Faye Wetherow** we explored future paths and possibilities for our work (or fun) we have been doing together. David and Faye are independent facilitators with a long history of involvement in the community living movement. They use a variety of facilitation tools including a graphic planning method called PATH (Planning Alternate Tomorrows with Hope). The purpose of PATH is to create more just, more hospitable, and more competent communities — a little bit at a time.

By the end of the day, we had helped **David** and **Faye** to create a huge mural filled with beautiful circle drawings that covered an entire wall. Then, one of the participants, **Ariane Templeton**, went home and drew some more pictures. Together, these circle drawings (you have seen some of them throughout the book) and the ideas we shared make up a visionary dream of a world where everyone is included and makes valued contributions.

Faye: *Dreams can be very big. They don't have to be achievable in the usual human sense. They hold the heart of our desires. Sometimes we call this a vision and sometimes we call this a dream. We need both our intellectual thinking and minds to create visions as well as our dreams that are connected to our hearts, our energy, and our spirits. I want to ask each of you about what your dream is, what is your vision?*

Linda: *My dream is a community where, when somebody meets somebody who is different (from a different culture, or has a different way of communicating, or thinks differently, or behaves differently, or gets around differently), that we would get excited about that difference rather than being afraid and that we would get curious and interested to learn more.*

Mark T.: *My dream would be a barrierless society. If you wish to close your eyes to see whatever you define as a barrier being smoothed out, or raised higher so that people could get around it easier: Levelled, ramped, sloped, Signed, communicated from the heart. The walls that separate us from our neighbours and from the world around us to be lowered.*

Mark M.: *What is important to me is communication. Not at a very basic level, but communication that really connects people. It doesn't have to be English, but communication that brings us together. It could be sign language, it could be spoken, or written. It doesn't matter what kind of communication. It doesn't matter if you are Hearing or Deaf, but communication is vital to me to make us equal.*

Glen: *My dream or vision for a community would be one that is more sensitive to other people's needs and dreams. People are so vulnerable and isolated. There needs to be more time in our communities for people to share. So many people are rushing around really stressed out, and so it's hard to be sensitive towards other people when people are experiencing a lot of stress, whatever that might be caused by. So just more quality time where we don't have to worry about all the material things that people are working towards.*

Tammy: *The quality of my dream is childlike. What I see in children is unconditional acceptance for all, back to the basics of simplicity where there is sharing and love for one another.*

Michael: *To have hope and strength and be brave. To show them. To communicate. Everybody laughing.*

Faye: *I think that is your gift Michael, I think you inspire people in that way. That is the sense I'm getting from you.*

Michael: *I work at Providence Farm with plants, once a week for a few weeks now on Fridays. I work doing planting. I smooth out the soil until it's perfect and all the seeds are in their place so they can grow. It's a lot better than before when things were pretty awful for me. Just staying with the planting.*

Andy: *I was born and grew up Hearing, until age 5 when I had an accident. Four months later when I started walking again I was very weak and in pain all over my body, including my spine which had been dislocated. I had to practice and retrain myself how to walk. By the time I was 17 years old I was able to run. I had gotten to that point through all my practice and exercising. I dreamt about Jesus and prayed to Jesus and a vision came to me of the whole world becoming as small as the tip of my little finger. Jesus was bigger than everything and was holding all of us in his hand. And he placed us all in my heart which expanded to encompass the whole world.*

Bob: *My wife and I are Deaf and my children and grandchildren are Hearing. We have a Grandson who is one and a half years old now. His parents are now teaching him Sign Language and we notice how quickly he is developing his Signing abilities. He is doing Sign Language better than he is actually speaking now. When I watch my Grandson, it makes me think about prehistoric times when the first language of the cavemen was a visual one. They communicated with their hands first and voice came much later. It feels good to think that the first language of the world was Sign Language and that it has influenced all the spoken languages as well.*

My thoughts...

....

....

....

....

....

....

....

....

....

....

....

....

....

....

....

....

....

....

....

....

....

....

Susan: *My dream of the future is to have interaction all together where we share. I dream that all these people are able to experience and share together while respecting each other's different cultures and languages. Attitudes and awareness are the keys I think. Being open and not closed minded in any sense. Being completely open to sharing and learning from each other. My dream is that all of us would be able to do that and not be concerned about war, land colonization, and all of that. I would hope to get a ticket to fly to have a taste of all different cultures for three months at time. I'd go to each different local area and experience, taste, and touch all those experiences that each culture has. I'm very interested in Australian culture and also disability cultures. I'd like to visit all the different Schools for the Deaf, to be able to go around and experience all the different languages throughout the world that Deaf people use.*

Gordon: *I guess one of my dreams is to show people what they can do instead of saying that they can't do it. I've been doing that a long time, especially with people who are mentally and physically handicapped. People who others said would never learn are now speaking. I had some great experiences recently in my church where the kids actually asked why I wear glasses and why I have a scooter. That was a great experience for me. I loved to tell them. I don't hide anything from children. If children want to know, they should know. We'll be teaching that there are differences but there are no differences because everyone here is a human being.*

My thoughts...

. . . .
. . . .
. . . .
. . . .
. . . .
. . . .
. . . .
. . . .
. . . .
. . . .
. . . .
. . . .
. . . .
. . . .
. . . .
. . . .
. . . .
. . . .
. . . .
. . . .
. . . .
. . . .
. . . .
. . . .

©1998 Linda D. Hill
Please obtain permission from the publisher to copy any page.
Building Bridges
Box 156, Duncan, British Columbia, CANADA V9L 3X3
Phone or fax toll free: 1-888-746-1529   TTY: 1-250-746-1539

Dianne: *My dream includes respect for each other. I think sometimes we think we are helping when actually we aren't. We need to remember respect. Also, choice. I think sometimes we do more harm than we mean to. So we need to remember respect and true choice.*

Lynn: *I close my eyes and I imagine the earth is one country and mankind its citizens. I think that for me the image would be that of a garden and that every single human being on that planet earth is a flower in that garden. For a garden to be truly beautiful it has a great variety of colours, smells, sizes, and shapes. Some grow best in the shade, others grow best in the sun. When they are all placed where they belong, then this garden is one that you just want to spend your whole life in. I imagine that some day, everybody will see everybody else as a different flower from that garden. I would like to see included as well the quality of laughter and happiness.*

Lynn: *Kevin would probably want to see the whole earth as a bowling alley.*
Kevin: *Yeah.* (with laughter)
Faye: *I know when you came in Kevin you expressed a lot of affection for people. That was very beautiful and welcoming.*
Lynn: *Kevin is very sensitive when somebody is hurt. You would like a world where no one ever felt sad, right Kevin?*
Kevin: *Yeah.*
Lynn: *I'm watching and trying to think if I could experience what Kevin is showing. I think that Kevin would love a world in which he could walk in to it and be understood or at least people would try to understand. I would suspect that that would be pretty cool, right Kevin? When Kevin holds up his hands for a Sign then people would know what he wants.*

Judi: *I would say that the thing I think about mostly is choice. Like the choice to understand people. There has to be a way that we could communicate. I think music is a universal language that everybody responds to, even those who we think are Deaf can hear and feel the beat and join right in.*

Bob: *Yes, we can feel the beat.* (Laughing) *I can also dance to the beat of a washing machine!*

Judi: *I think that the quality that is more important than almost anything is openness. I was always very much afraid to let people know that I was in any way handicapped. I would say, "Thank you very much, I am not." But I am, I know I am, there is no question in that. But I would tell people they didn't need to open the door for me. "I can do it myself, thank you very much." But I got told off in grand style by a number of people and I learned that if you say "No, It's OK. I can do it.", they are not going to help the person who comes later, who can't. They'll say, "Oh well, that other person said 'forget it,' so I don't need to, so I'm not going to try again." But being open makes people realize that it makes you feel good to help.*

My thoughts...

Andrew: *I want to work full time, all day and have fun at night like playing pool and stuff.*

Erik: *My life has been a roller coaster. What I have learned over this past couple of years is that we need to have friends, friends we can call on.*

Jim: *For the future my dream is to have a farm, to be riding on horseback, and to go on hikes — everything. To smell the forest, and the trees, and enjoy the beauty everywhere I look. A ranch with cows would be great. One really great dream is the wish to go camping, sleep in sleeping bags, build a fire and sit around it like Indians. That's my dream.*

My thoughts...

· · · · · · · · · · · · · · · · · · · ·

· · · · · · · · · · · · · · · · · · · ·

· · · · · · · · · · · · · · · · · · · ·

· · · · · · · · · · · · · · · · · · · ·

· · · · · · · · · · · · · · · · · · · ·

· · · · · · · · · · · · · · · · · · · ·

· · · · · · · · · · · · · · · · · · · ·

· · · · · · · · · · · · · · · · · · · ·

· · · · · · · · · · · · · · · · · · · ·

· · · · · · · · · · · · · · · · · · · ·

· · · · · · · · · · · · · · · · · · · ·

· · · · · · · · · · · · · · · · · · · ·

· · · · · · · · · · · · · · · · · · · ·

· · · · · · · · · · · · · · · · · · · ·

· · · · · · · · · · · · · · · · · · · ·

· · · · · · · · · · · · · · · · · · · ·

· · · · · · · · · · · · · · · · · · · ·

· · · · · · · · · · · · · · · · · · · ·

· · · · · · · · · · · · · · · · · · · ·

· · · · · · · · · · · · · · · · · · · ·

Lorne: *I want to see lots more people and different faces every day of the week.*

Jack: *In our day program we've been working on communication through pictures, blocks, PIC symbols, and stuff like that so the guys can see what their day is set up for, and then they can go and do those things. I would just like to see that continue and strengthen in such a way that the fellows could communicate in such a way that their needs would be met always and express themselves without the guesses.*

Glen: *I think our society is driven too much by money. What a lot of people have in this room is time and appreciation for the simple things like going for walks in the woods and by the ocean. Things that too many people who are working and chasing money have forgotten. So, in my dream each person has to think. "Where can I meet someone who is not paid to provide services but someone in the community?" Maybe it is someone at church or someone down the street. They would take turns doing that and then the groups would get bigger and bigger. And because they could share the appreciation for the simple things in life, the attitudes of the people in the community busy working all the time would start to change.*

Arianne: *I have many visions. I have a vision to create because I'm an artist. I have a vision to play the flute as well as playing the piano. My vision is just to walk in the forest and see the sun glowing through the trees and to communicate with my friends.*

David: *You've been talking about seeing differences as learning opportunities and gifts not as barriers. The kinds of interests, passions, and gifts that people have around the ocean, camping, nature, hiking, and creating! Touching and tasting all different cultures and languages. All of that coming alive in a context of friendship, communication, respect, and openness. Deepening friendships. Deepening meanings. Sharing and learning from each other. Feeling safe with each other. Out of that are coming these experiences of choice and the sun glowing through the trees, flowers in the garden of humanity.*

BUILDING BRIDGES

©1998 Linda D. Hill
Please obtain permission from the publisher to copy any page.
Building Bridges
Box 156, Duncan, British Columbia, CANADA V9L 3X3
Phone or fax toll free: 1-888-746-1529   TTY: 1-250-746-1539

For Further Reading

A few books and national or international magazines that have more ideas about bridging disability differences:

Ability Network Publishing Inc. (since 1992) *Ability Network: Canada's cross-disability magazine.* Nova Scotia: Ability Network, PO Box 24045, 21 MicMac Blvd., Dartmouth, Nova Scotia, B3A 4T4.

Arnold, R., Burke, B., James, C., Martin, D., Thomas, B. (1991) *Educating for a Change.* Ontario: Between the Lines and the Doris Marshall Institute for Education and Action.

Banks, J. (1994) *All of Us Together: The Story of Inclusion at the Kinzie School.* Washington, DC: Gallaudet University Press.

Canadian Abilities Foundation (since 1988) *Abilities: Canada's lifestyle magazine for people with disabilities.* Ontario: Canadian Abilities Foundation, 444 Yonge Street, Toronto, Ontario, M5S 1T1.

Condeluci, A. (1991) *Interdependence: The Route to Community.* Florida: Paul M. Deutsch Press Inc.

Disabled Peoples International (since 1993) *Disability International.* Manitoba: Disabled Peoples International, 101-7 Evergreen Place, Winnipeg, Manitoba, R3L 2T3

Falvey, M., Forest, M., Pearpoint, J., and Rosenberg, R. (1995) *All My Life's a Circle: Using the tools Circles, MAPS and PATH.* Ontario: Inclusion Press International.

Hutchison, P. and McGill, J. (1992) *Leisure, Integration and Community.* Ontario: Leisurability Publications Inc.

Perske, R. and Perske, M. (1988) *Circles of Friends: People with disabilities and their friends enrich the lives of one another.* Ontario: Welch Publishing Company Ltd.

Roeher Institute (1989) *The Pursuit of Leisure: Enriching the lives of people who have a disability.* Ontario: The G. Allan Roeher Institute, York University, Kinsmen Building, 4700 Keele Street, North York, Ontario, M3J 1P3.

Roeher Institute (since 1985) *Entourage: How people can be supported by the community to live, learn, work, and have fun in the community.* Ontario: The G. Allan Roeher Institute.

Schwartz, D. (1992) *Crossing the River: Creating a Conceptual Revolution in Community and Disability.* Massachusetts: Brookline Books.

(cont'd)

My thoughts...

For Further Reading (cont'd)

Stone, K. (1997) *Awakening to Disability: Nothing about us without us.*
California: Volcano Press.

Walsh, A. (Editor) (1992) *The Real Guide. Able to Travel: True stories by and for people with disabilities.* New York: Prentice Hall Travel.

Werner, D. (1987) *Disabled Village Children: A guide for community health workers, rehabilitation workers, and families.* California: The Hesperian Foundation, P. O. Box 1692, Palo Alto, CA, 94302, USA.

Wetherow, D. (Editor) (1992) *The Whole Community Catalogue: Welcoming people with disabilities into the heart of community life.* Manitoba: Gunnars and Campbell, 209-1844 Pembina Highway, Winnipeg, R3T 2G2. Connecticut: Communitas, Box 374, Manchester, Connecticut 06040.

My thoughts...

. . . .

. . . .

. . . .

. . . .

. . . .

. . . .

. . . .

. . . .

. . . .

. . . .

. . . .

. . . .

. . . .

. . . .

. . . .

. . . .

. . . .

. . . .

. . . .

. . . .

. . . .

. . . .

. . . .

. . . .

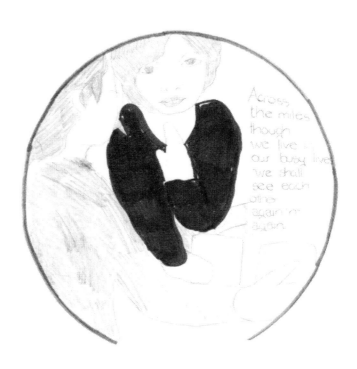

Discovering Connections in action
— *illustration by*
Ariane Templeton

©1998 Linda D. Hill
Please obtain permission from the publisher to copy any page.
Building Bridges
Box 156, Duncan, British Columbia, CANADA V9L 3X3
Phone or fax toll free: 1-888-746-1529 TTY: 1-250-746-1539

About The Author

Linda Hill, Ph.D. is a registered psychologist, and a family member of an individual who lives with disabilities. She has been involved in disability rights, community development, and social justice work for over twenty years.

"My focus is on finding positive, creative ways to build healthy connections in ourselves, our families, and our communities. Each positive and peaceful action one of us takes shows the way for many other people who are looking for hope and leadership."

Linda has enjoyed years of collaborative association with several non-profit societies including: Island Deaf and Hard of Hearing Centre, her local Association for Community Living, Canadian Mental Health Association, as well as the Cowichan Valley Independent Living Resource Centre whose members helped her write ***Discovering Connections***.

Linda and her husband, **John Scull**, are also active members of several environmental and social justice groups. They recently spent two years as CUSO cooperants, living and working in the Solomon Islands where Linda helped government and non-government disability organizations develop community-based rehabilitation services. ***Discovering Connections*** is the first of several projects Linda and John are publishing together in their ***Building Bridges Consulting*** work. When they are not working or travelling, Linda and John enjoy spending time with family, walking on the beach, and messing about in small sailing boats near their home in Maple Bay.

Contact Linda at:

Building Bridges
P.O. Box 156, Duncan, BC, Canada, V9L 3X3
Phone or Fax : 1-250-746-1529 or
in Canada and USA phone or fax toll free: 1-888-746-1529
TTY: 1-250-746-1539
E-mail: BRIDGES@ISLAND.NET
Visit our web page at: http://www.island.net/~bridges/

Deb Thorne and Cathy La France

About The Cowichan Valley Independent Living Resource Centre

The Cowichan Valley Independent Living Resource Centre offers a variety of programs that assist persons with disabilities to achieve the goal of Independent Living. The Resource Centre uses a community development approach to work towards creating a healthy and inclusive community that is accessible to, and accepting of all it's citizens. Consumer control ensures that disabled persons participate in the governance and operation of this organization. A cross-disability focus enables the organization to address the needs of people with any type of disability. Being community based means the Independent Living Resource Centre responds to the needs of the community. Promoting integration and full participation creates a caring community that welcomes all its citizens. Participating in the Canadian Association of Independent Living Centres supports the development of the Independent Living Movement across Canada. **Cathy La France** has been Executive Director of the Resource Centre since it was incorporated as a non-profit society on August 17, 1990. **Deb Thorne** coordinates peer support and applies *Discovering Connections* daily in her work and play.

The Resource Centre provides information and support to people with disabilities, family members, friends, and individuals interested in supporting people with disabilities. The Centre offers information and referral, parking placards, peer support, independent living skills training, as well as research and development of Independent Living Services.

Cathy, Deb and their colleagues can be contacted at:

Cowichan Valley Independent Living Resource Centre
#2 – 5855 York Road, Duncan, BC, Canada, V9L 3S3
Phone (voice or TTY): 250-746-3930, Fax: 250-746-3662
E-mail: cvilrc@cowichan.com
Web Site:http://www.cowichan.com/business/cvilrc/index.htm

BUILDING
BRIDGES

©1998 Linda D. Hill
Please obtain permission from the publisher to copy any page.
Building Bridges
Box 156, Duncan, British Columbia, CANADA V9L 3X3
Phone or fax toll free: 1-888-746-1529   TTY: 1-250-746-1539

About The Artists

Ian Finlayson . . . .

Ian Finlayson studied at Sheridan College in Oakville, Ontario, and has worked as a professional illustrator and designer, within the graphic arts industry, for more than fifteen years. For this project Ian has employed an expressive, pen and ink line technique complimented with soft watercolour washes. Ian lives with his family in Cobble Hill, British Columbia, and can be reached by E-mail at finlyson@islandnet.com

Kim Barnard . . . .

Kim Barnard is a home-based computer graphic artist who operates her business, Graphic Details, in the picturesque surroundings of Shawnigan Lake, BC. With close to 10 years of experience working in trade shops from Vancouver to Victoria, Kim is pleased to bring her skills to bear in helping to communicate the thoughts and ideas contained in this guidebook. "More than words on paper," she explains, "is what you will find within." Reach Kim at Graphic Details, Phone: 250-743-1785, Fax: 250-743-1781

David and Faye Wetherow . . . .

David and Faye Wetherow are independent facilitators, trainers and consultants who use and teach a variety of creative facilitation tools including PATH, the Stone Game, Solution Circles, and Foundations Training. They share their lives with Faye's adopted daughter, Amber, who faces significant mobility and communication challenges. Faye and David can be reached at The Community Institute, 911 Terrien Way, Parksville, BC, V9P 1T2. Phone: 250-248-2531, Cellular: 250-248-1714, Fax: 250-248-2685 E-mail: wetherow@bcsupernet.com

Ariane Templeton . . . .

Ariane Colleen Templeton is a self-taught artist who was drawing before she learned to walk. "I remember filling tons of jumbo pads with my drawings when I was younger. I listen to music while I draw and the music is my inspiration. I hope that my art makes people feel happy. That's why I do it!" Ariane lives in the L'Arche Victoria community. Ariane can be reached through L'Arche Victoria, 1640 Gladstone Avenue, Victoria, BC, V8R 1S7 Phone: 250-595-1014, E-mail: larche@bcl.com

Building Bridges
To Other Communities

Linda and her husband **John** give workshops on a wide variety of disability and cross-cultural communication topics as well as supporting culturally-sensitive organizational and community development. Their involvement in disability issues, international development, and land conservation has taken them throughout British Columbia, elsewhere in Canada, and the South Pacific. **Cathy La France** and her colleagues in the Cowichan Valley Independent Living Resource Centre are recognized nationally for their leadership work reducing violence against people with disabilities. **David** and **Faye Wetherow** help families, agencies, and community groups throughout the USA and Canada develop value-based action plans, strengthen relationships and work towards inclusive communities.

We each have a vision of an interconnected world where every living being's gifts are acknowledged, supported, and valued and where we all share in our caring for each other and for our Earth. Each of us enjoys travelling and giving workshops. We look forward to opportunities to provide training and consultation in more communities.

©1998 Linda D. Hill
Please obtain permission from the publisher to copy any page.
Building Bridges
Box 156, Duncan, British Columbia, CANADA V9L 3X3
Phone or fax toll free: 1-888-746-1529   TTY: 1-250-746-1539

BUILDING
BRIDGES

Discovering Connections in action

— illustrations by
David & Faye Wetherow

Building Bridges
Box 156, Duncan, British Columbia, CANADA V9L 3X3
Phone or fax toll free: **1-888-746-1529** TTY: **1-250-746-1539**